Motivating Yourself for Achievement

Motivating Yourself for Achievement

ARTHUR H. BELL, PH.D.

DAYLE M. SMITH, PH.D.

School of Business and Management
University of San Francisco

NetEffect Series

Upper Saddle River, New Jersey
Columbus, Ohio

Library of Congress Cataloging-in-Publication Data

Bell, Arthur H. (Arthur Henry)
    Motivating yourself for achievement / Arthur H. Bell and Dayle M. Smith.
      p. cm.
    Includes bibliographical references.
    ISBN 0-13-033542-8
    1. Achievement motivation. I. Smith, Dayle M. II. Title.
    BF503 .B45 2003
    153.8—dc21

                                                  2002021853

Vice President and Publisher: Jeffery W. Johnston
Senior Acquisitions Editor: Sande Johnson
Assistant Editor: Cecilia Johnson
Production Editor: JoEllen Gohr
Production Coordination: BookMasters, Inc.
Design Coordinator: Diane C. Lorenzo
Cover Designer: Ceri Fitzgerald
Cover Art: Corbis Stock Market
Production Manager: Pamela D. Bennett
Director of Marketing: Ann Castel Davis
Director of Advertising: Kevin Flanagan
Marketing Manager: Christina Quadhamer

This book was set in Goudy by BookMasters, Inc. It was printed and bound by Hamilton Printing. The cover was printed by Phoenix Color Corp.

Pearson Education Ltd.
Pearson Education Australia Pty. Limited
Pearson Education Singapore Pte. Ltd.
Pearson Education North Asia Ltd.
Pearson Education Canada, Ltd.
Pearson Educación de Mexico, S.A. de C.V.
Pearson Education—Japan
Pearson Education Malaysia Pte. Ltd.
Pearson Education, *Upper Saddle River, New Jersey*

10 9 8 7 6 5 4 3 2

ISBN 0-13-033542-8

We dedicate this book with love and admiration to our children, Art, Lauren, and Maddie. They motivate us in ways they will never know.

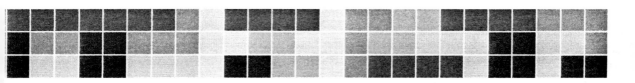

Contents

Preface

Over the centuries, professions have arisen to serve almost every human need. Literally every inch from our head to our toes has its specialist or practitioner. Similarly, machines and technologies have entire industries committed to their creation, maintenance, and improvement. It is especially surprising, therefore, that no mainstream professional group has come forward to inform us about and assist us with a prime mover in human affairs: how to motivate oneself to achievement.

The highly individual art of thinking thoughts or engaging in activities that get one off the couch and into action remains largely self-learned, or never learned. In this short book on a vastly important topic, we speak to those already involved in their careers, as well as those preparing for the world of work. We attempt to summarize the most valuable streams of research and information about motivation in ways that are interesting and directly applicable to school or work life.

To motivate your passion for this topic, we provide many "Your Turn" opportunities throughout the book for your insights, comments, questions, objections, and feedback. A series of more than 80 "Insights" help the main ideas of the book stand out. A statement of chapter goals and a chapter-end summary support this same goal.

Our earnest wish for this book is that it will serve to awaken and broaden your thoughts and feelings about personal motivators that can stimulate action and encourage meaningful action throughout your career.

ACKNOWLEDGMENTS

The desire to write about motivation springs primarily from our gratitude to the many individuals who have taught us, shown us, chided us, praised us, and befriended us over the years. These people dot the academic as well as the corporate landscape around the world. They are all beacons of motivation to those with whom they work and to those they serve.

Executives and managers at more than 100 companies and organizations helped shape our insights on motivation at work. Special thanks go to leaders at Price-waterhouse Coopers, PaineWebber, TRW, Lockheed Martin, Citicorp, Sun Microsystems, Charles Schwab, Genentech, American Stores, Cost Plus World Market, China Resources, Guangdong Enterprises, U.S. State Department, Colonial Williamsburg Foundation, U.S. Central Intelligence Agency, U.S. Coast Guard, New York Life Insurance, IBM, Pacific Bell, British Telecommunications, Deutsche Telekom, and Cushman Wakefield.

We also thank many supportive colleagues and friends at the University of Southern California, Naval Postgraduate School, Georgetown University, and the School of Business and Management at the University of San Francisco.

We are indebted to the insights and influence over the years of our esteemed academic colleagues: Professors Tom Housel, Bill Murray, Zhan Li, Les Myers, Steve Alter, Karl Boedecker, Barry Doyle, Steve Calvert, Joel Oberstone, Peggy Takahashi, Heather Cowan, Caren Siehl, Dave Bowen, Mary Ann von Glinow, Norman Sigband, Doug McCabe, Denis Neilson, Steve Huxley, Alev Efendioglu, Heather Hudson, Roger Chen, Richard Puntillo, Eugene Muscat, Salvadore Aceves, Rex Bennett, Todd Sayre, Mark Cannice, Mike Middleton, Sheryl Barker, Cathy Fusco, Dan Blakley, Carol Graham, and Dean Gary Williams.

Arthur H. Bell
Dayle M. Smith

Belvedere, California

OTHER BOOKS IN THIS SERIES BY BELL/SMITH

Learning Team Skills
Managing Your Time
Interviewing for Success
Building Your Network
Developing Leadership Abilities

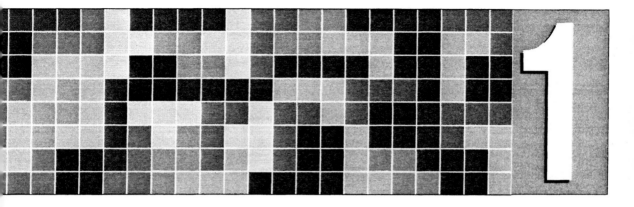

Motivation: What It Is—and Isn't

GOALS

- Understand a working definition of motivation.
- Confine the scope of this discussion of motivation to personal motivators.
- Recognize the highly individualistic nature of motivation.
- Conduct an overview of major forms of personal motivators.

Like other books in this series, *Motivating Yourself for Achievement* is more a conversation than a lecture. At frequent points during your reading, you will have the opportunity to record your own thoughts, reactions, questions, and comments. As authors, we hope you will seize these chances to participate in attaining the overall goal of the book: to understand what motivates you—and how you can access those motivators when you need them.

This book is somewhat unique in restricting its focus solely to you and your motivators. A quick scan of book titles on motivation on the Internet or in bookstores will show that the majority of books on this topic deal with motivating others. These books often are aimed at managers and supervisors whose success depends upon their ability to "build a fire" under employees in order to accomplish company goals.

This book, however, turns the spotlight on you. By discussing and giving examples of many forms of motivation, we want to help you examine your own set of usual motivators. In addition, we hope to awaken you to a new or underdeveloped set of motivators that might serve you well in the future.

So that the communication begun in this book is not completely one-sided, we would be happy to hear from you about your experiences and experiments with personal motivators. Whatever you write to us will be treated confidentially. It would be our privilege to learn what works and doesn't work for you among the dozens of motivators described in this book. You can e-mail the authors at bell@usfca.edu.

In this book, an insight is introduced, followed by a series of questions under the heading "Your Turn." These questions are designed to give you a chance to examine your own way of handling each issue. Next comes a short discussion of the specific insight. In some chapters the discussion precedes the insight statement. Let's get started.

INSIGHT 1	Knowing what motivates us puts us in control of the activities, commitments, and involvements we decide to take on.

Your Turn	

Describe ways you have tended to motivate yourself in the past. What are some of the forces that lead you to say "yes" to challenges and opportunities?

WHAT MOTIVATES YOU?

Before delving into definitions and examples of motivation, let's take an immediate case: You hold in your hand a short book—*Motivating Yourself for Achievement*—which we would very much like you to read. What motivates you to do so?

If you have acquired the book as part of a college or company class or training session, you might be motivated to read by your desire to follow the instructions of your professor or boss. "I have to read the book to pass the class," you might be saying to yourself. In addition, you might be motivated by your interest in the subject itself. "I know I need a motivational push once in a while. Maybe this book can help me."

Money could play a part in your motivation. "I paid for the book and I can only get my money's worth by reading it." Curiosity also can be a motivator as you skim the chapter titles. "I wonder what expectancy motivation is. What are demotivators?"

We could speculate on many other internal and external forces that influence your decision whether or not to read this book. The point is that something motivates your actions in the case of your reading and in all the other large and small decisions you make. The achievements you ultimately attain in your personal and professional life depend directly upon your motivators. Getting to know what has motivated you so far can help you understand your wins and losses to date. Getting to know new motivators can help you add to the win column as you move ahead in your academic and work life.

Virtually every act we find ourselves engaged in stems from personal motivation in some form.	**INSIGHT 2**

Your Turn
You are now reading this book. What motivates you to do so? Make an effort to think deeply about the obvious and not-so-obvious personal motivators that keep you turning these pages.

MOTIVATION: A CURRENT, NOT A SWITCH

The root meaning of the term *motivation* involves *movement*, as expressed in words such as *automotive*, *locomotion*, and *emotion* (being "moved"). Cars, trains, and planes notwithstanding, motivation for human beings does not begin with the turning of a key or the flipping of a switch. The notion that a magic phrase or thought can turn us on instantly to energetic endeavor is pure Hollywood. In fact, no one is so robotic that a motivational mantra or switch can be flipped (by ourselves or others) to set us into sustained, purposeful action. Phrases such as "I think I can, I think I can" (from *The Little Engine that Could*) make good children's stories but poor sources of reliable motivation for real life. This book, therefore, is not about mental tricks you can play on yourself in an attempt to gain the advantages of increased motivation. If motivational tricks worked, you would have discovered them by now and so would we.

Unlike a switch to be flipped, human motivation is much more akin to a reliable energy source. The nature of that energy varies for each person and for each of the many kinds of challenges, tasks, and activities we face. The overarching purpose of this book is to help you discover "outlets" that you can tap into for a surge of motivational energy suited to your personality and circumstances.

INSIGHT 3	Personal motivation is not a matter of tricking ourselves into particular beliefs or attitudes.

Your Turn

Describe one source of motivation that has proven to be a reliable energy source for you when you've needed a push to get started with projects and activities. Tell why you think this particular source of motivation has been important for you.

THE SCIENCE AND ART OF MOTIVATION

A science demands that phenomena be studied in an objective, observable, and repeatable way. The frog you dissected in high school biology wasn't a matter of opinion; organs and other structures were plainly there to observe, record data about, and slip into your lab partner's backpack.

Since the early 1900s, human motivation has been investigated scientifically. Test and control groups have been established in hundreds of carefully designed experiments to understand how particular motivational stimuli influence individuals and groups. Among the earliest of these experiments were the famous "Hawthorne Effect" investigations of Harvard Professor Elton Mayo. He sought to understand the physical (and, as it turned out, mental) factors that promoted superior performance among factory workers. (Many of the scientific efforts to understand human motivation are described in the works cited in the Recommended Reading section of this book.)

By contrast, an art allows subjective impressions and feelings that cannot be tested or proven by scientific methods. For example, the artistic techniques of Michelangelo are deeply moving to some people and not to others. Art, as the saying goes, is in the eye of the beholder. Similarly, we are each artists when it comes to our selection and use of self-motivators. Like any art, the art of personal motivation remains largely mysterious: We can't always say why we are powerfully motivated by a particular idea or goal on one day and not on another. We often find the whole matter of personal motivation frustrating indeed. We can't predict over time what motivators will work best to spur us on to particular activities or achievements. That lack of predictability along with our subjective interpretation of motivating influences makes motivation as much an art as a science. From the palette of many possible motivators, we dip in our brush and paint the path of our future actions. Your picture will differ from ours, and it should.

Much scientific information is known about human motivation. However, its application in our thinking and feeling remains more an art than a science.	**INSIGHT 4**

Your Turn
Tell about a time when your usual sources of motivation failed to rouse you for an activity or experience of some kind. What did you do? How did things turn out?

A BASELINE EXPERIMENT: YOU AT REPOSE

As an overview of the major themes of this book, we can walk through various types of motivation—and demotivation—by imagining a familiar scenario: You wake up on a Saturday morning. Let's consider eight common motivators that might get you out of bed and into your day.

Motivation by physical need. If you're hungry or need to use the bathroom, you probably will resist the temptation to pull up the covers for another hour or two of sleep. Although we seldom give them much thought, such physical motivators are responsible for a great deal of what we find ourselves doing during an ordinary day.

Our most common physical needs and feelings play a major role in determining what we do each day.	**INSIGHT 5**

Your Turn
Describe your own experience of hunger as a major motivator during an average day. When does it exert its influence most powerfully? What happens when you try to ignore it?

Motivation by habit. Perhaps you have made it your daily practice to jump out of bed for a quick round of calisthenics or a morning jog. Habits motivate many of our most familiar daily activities, including brushing teeth, washing dishes, feeding the dog or cat, picking up the mail or newspaper, and a host of other subconscious acts.

INSIGHT 6	We each have "habits of mind" that lead us into activity almost without our knowing it.

Your Turn	
Discuss one or more of your habitual motivators. Where did these habits come from?	

Motivation by the pursuit of pleasure. You leap out of bed in this case because you are motivated by two tickets to attend the Big Game with a friend. You've been looking forward to this day for weeks. Your burst of energy as you dress, eat, and hurry out the door stems from your desire to enjoy every minute of the long-awaited sports experience.

INSIGHT 7	We respond powerfully and enthusiastically to motivators that promise pleasure.

Your Turn	
Tell about a recent time when you were motivated by the pursuit of pleasure involving a sporting event, a music event, or a similar occasion. When did you first feel the motivation? How did you respond?	

Motivation by the avoidance of pain. You get out of bed because your drill sergeant, mother, or significant other (take your pick) will badger you verbally if you attempt to sleep in. Under threat of punishment (however mild or subtle), we find ourselves influenced and somewhat energized to act. If the threatened punishment is severe (for example, losing your job for being late), the motivation to avoid such pain can be strong indeed.

Pain or the threat of pain motivates us to act in a way that lessens or avoids the pain.	**INSIGHT 8**

	Your Turn
Describe at least one pain or threat-of-pain motivator in your present life. Is it a useful motivator for you or do you wish that you could rid yourself of it?	

Motivation by association. Let's say that everyone in the house gets up between 6:30 A.M. and 7:00 A.M. and you do, too. People in groups, whether organized as a family, a team, a convent, or an army troop, often fall into the same general rhythms of life when it comes to eating, sleeping, scheduling leisure time, and other activities. "Everyone's doing it," we say to ourselves, "and I'd rather fall in than fall out when it comes to my group."

The example of others, for better or worse, exerts a strong motivational influence on us.	**INSIGHT 9**

	Your Turn
Consider your social group at school or work. Discuss one or two activities that you were motivated to undertake primarily because the group did so, as well. Why do you think motivation by association is so powerful?	

Motivation by belief and conviction. At least a few of your ancestors probably believed the saying "early to bed, early to rise, makes a man healthy, wealthy, and wise." They got out of bed motivated by their beliefs (much as many people now take vitamins or follow other regimens in the firm conviction that these measures promote good health).

What we believe about ourselves, others, and the world itself motivates us to act or not act in certain ways.	**INSIGHT 10**

Your Turn

Choose one of your main beliefs or values. Then discuss how this conviction motivates you in social, school, or work circumstances.

Motivation by a sense of equity. Children might not be in your future plans, but imagine this situation: Your spouse climbs out of bed to start the process of feeding and dressing the kids. Although your spouse hasn't pressured you in any direct way to get out of bed, you feel that fairness requires you to (groan) get up and do your share of the parenting activities.

INSIGHT 11   Our willingness to do our fair share stems from our conscious or unconscious sensitivity to justice in human activities and relationships.

Your Turn

Tell about a time when you were motivated by your sense of fairness to perform a particular activity or engage in an experience of some kind.

Motivation by expectation. We each have public and private hopes for our individual futures. You might have announced publicly that you want to go to law school someday. Privately, you might have dreams of affluence and influence from your eventual career opportunities. Taken together, these expectations can operate as powerful motivators. "If I ever want to be a lawyer," you might say to yourself, "I'd better get out of bed and hit the books."

INSIGHT 12   We act today as if we knew what was coming tomorrow.

Your Turn

Choose one important thing you are expecting in the short- or long-term future. What does this expectation motivate you to do in your present life?

WHEN MOTIVATORS FAIL ENTIRELY

So you're still in bed? Everyone has experienced times when the traditional motivators mentioned just don't have the power to rouse us from inactivity. Assuming you are well rested, such malaise can become medically significant if it continues over a week or more or recurs in a chronic way. Health experts estimate that up to 20 percent of Americans will experience at least one bout with depression during their lifetimes. The common symptoms of depression are feelings of hopelessness and an inability to undertake the usual activities of daily life. Many people suffering from depression literally pull the bedcovers over their head and want the world to go away.

Here is a well-known set of symptoms used by physicians and mental health professionals to determine whether depressive feelings are significant enough to warrant treatment as an illness. This battery of symptoms is included not to worry you about common feelings of "the blahs," but instead to make you aware that the failure of virtually all personal motivators can be an indication of depressive illness. Fortunately, clinical depression is highly treatable. If you suspect that your own experience with prolonged periods of inactivity, profound sadness, or other clusters of symptoms on the list are in fact signs of depression, we urge you to talk through your situation with a doctor.

Note that no single symptom on this list automatically signals a diagnosis of depression. The nature, severity, and duration of many symptoms are considered by doctors in deciding whether or not depression is present. Among these symptoms are:

- Reduced interest in activities.
- Indecisiveness.
- Perpetual or recurring feelings of sadness.
- Irritability.
- Getting too much or too little sleep.
- Loss of concentration.
- Increased or decreased appetite.
- Loss of self-esteem.
- Decreased sexual desire.
- Problems with memory.
- Moods of despair and hopelessness.
- Suicidal thoughts.
- Reduced feelings of happiness and pleasure.
- Inescapable guilt feelings.
- Uncontrollable spells of crying.
- Feelings of helplessness.

- Restlessness.
- Feelings of disorganization.
- Difficulty doing daily tasks.
- Lack of energy, fatigue.
- Self-attacking thoughts.
- Feelings of being in a stupor.
- Nagging worries of disaster, financial ruin, or ill health.
- Feelings of being detached from one's immediate environment.

These and other common symptoms of depression are discussed in depth in *Overcoming Anxiety, Panic, and Depression* by James Gardner, M.D., et al. (Career Press, 2000). You also might want to investigate a Web site where sufferers from depression-related illnesses record their feelings and symptoms: www.moodswing.com.

INSIGHT 13	A chronic, debilitating lack of motivation might signal underlying physical or emotional maladies.

Your Turn	
If you have known a person who suffered from depression, describe what you remember of that person's main symptoms. If you do not know such a person, tell what you would do if you suspected that your own lack of motivation indicated possible depression.	

THE NATURAL RHYTHMS OF MOTIVATION

We do not want to give the impression that constant motivation is a good thing or a recommended goal. In fact, the goad to perpetual activity (manic behavior) is the flip side of depressive illness and, left untreated, results in the same destructive effects on an individual's life as lack of motivation.

The natural rhythms of life dictate in large part when motivators have their place and power. For example, sleep acts each day to turn off motivators for a period of 6 to 10 hours for most individuals. As we drift into slumber, we let go of thoughts of what we must do, should do, can do, and want to do. If we play those motivating thoughts over and over in our heads at bedtime, we may find ourselves up half the night. The condition of insomnia is associated in many individuals with an overactive mental "chatter" of stimulating hopes, worries, must-do lists, and so forth.

A second natural rhythm for motivation occurs in the work-rest cycle. Our days typically are made up of a series of tasks. In an office environment, these tasks often are grouped by time: We work solidly from 8 A.M. to 10 A.M., for example, and then take a short break before plunging back into work activity from 10:15 A.M. or so until noon. The same sort of time division organizes our work-rest rhythm for the afternoon.

In some cases, our rhythm for motivation might not depend on the clock at all, but instead on subdivisions of the task(s) at hand. If we are building a house, for example, we might decide to nail down the flooring in one of the bedrooms, then take a break before resuming with another portion of the construction. In these cases, we consciously decide to turn off personal motivators for a brief time (a break or lunch) while we rest from physical and/or mental exertion and gather our strength for continued work.

When these natural rhythms are out of whack in an individual, we define that person as a workaholic—that is, someone apparently plagued by unrelenting motivation and obsessed with pursuing work activity even to the detriment of health and happiness.

Motivation and rest or relaxation must coexist in balance.	**INSIGHT 14**

	Your Turn
Tell about a time when you felt you were too motivated or energized for activity. What was the end result?	

FINDING YOUR OWN RHYTHMS FOR REST AND MOTIVATION

One of the most important but least emphasized aspects of personal development lies in discovering the balance between rest and motivation that is uniquely right for you. School experiences from our earliest years do little to promote this self-discovery of balance. In school, we are taught (implicitly or explicitly) to suppress our individual feelings of when we require rest or diversion and when we are ready to be motivated to accomplish tasks. Classroom life proceeds by the clock and calendar (algebra from 9 A.M. to 10 A.M., term papers due on October 7, and so forth). If our own work-rest rhythm doesn't fit well with this pattern, we are labeled as poor students ('lazy,' 'tardy,' 'working below ability level').

Some individuals carry this school-induced mentality into their adult lives. They feel that something is wrong with them if they find it uncomfortable to maintain the same work schedule as their work associates. They blame themselves for lack of character, ambition, or stamina if their personal work-rest rhythms are at variance with those approved by management or typically practiced as part of company culture.

Certainly one of the most satisfying joys of attaining adult maturity (at whatever chronological age) is the personal resolution to listen to your own promptings regarding when to rest and when to be spurred to activity. Although few of us have the luxury to live entirely by our own impulses, we can tailor our adult lives to some degree so that our hours are filled more and more by what we want to do rather than by what we have to do.

Finding your individual balance between rest (including mental diversion) and motivated task activity has important implications for your health and happiness. Stress-related maladies and illnesses ranging from headaches to high blood pressure to ulcers all have their genesis at least in part in the frenetic schedules we attempt to keep in defiance of what our bodies are telling us. The notion of retirement is attractive for many American workers simply because it appears to offer relief from the rat race imposed by someone else's sense of how our time should be spent. We should not wait until our so-called golden years to discover and respect our individual requirements for balance between rest and work. That process—self-development in its truest form—should begin in childhood and proceed with increasing refinement and commitment throughout our lives.

INSIGHT 15	The balance we each create between motivation and rest in our lives is highly individual.

Your Turn

How would you describe the balance between motivation and rest or relaxation in your life? Does that balance change from time to time? If so, how and why?

LOCATING YOUR OWN SOURCES FOR MOTIVATION

The remainder of this book is a tour of likely sources for motivation and a cautionary "not-wanted" list of demotivators. No one source of motivation fits all personalities and circumstances. By considering each form of motivation discussed in these pages, you put yourself in a good position to select the right motivation source (or combination of sources) to help you achieve your goals.

Summing Up

The science and art of motivation, as it applies to our individual lives, requires our sensitivity to balance. Too much or too little motivation can ruin our healthy, satisfying engagement in activities and experiences. A chronic, debilitating lack of motivation could signal underlying depression and should be checked out with a physician. By locating our existing individual motivators and exploring other possible motivators, we put ourselves rather than others in the position of controlling our life decisions—large and small.

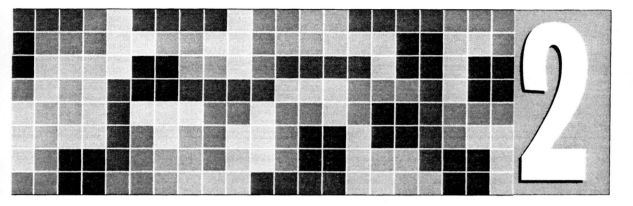

Dealing with the Classic Demotivators

GOALS

- Grasp the nature and influence of thoughts and ideas that rob us of motivation.

- Understand what gives these thoughts and ideas power over us.

- Gain insight into the flaws and deceptions at the heart of these demotivators.

It's often difficult to sort out when we want to do nothing at all and when we want to or need to undertake an activity of some kind. No inner alarm clock goes off to tell us that we've rested enough and now it's time to get busy in some way.

Instead, we go through an inner evaluation, consciously or unconsciously, that helps us make up our minds whether to continue to rest or set to work. We weigh a variety of thoughts and feelings (often in a matter of seconds) and come up with a verdict that determines our future course.

In the course of this evaluation, we inevitably deal with one or more of the "classic demotivators"—so called because they have effectively stalled action for countless human generations. We had to deal with several of these classic demotivators in undertaking the substantial task of writing this book; perhaps you also confronted one or more of the classic demotivators in your decision to read it.

These demotivators are not necessarily false in what they propose. Sometimes we call a demotivator to mind and find ourselves agreeing with it completely. However, more often the classic demotivators filter through our decision-making process as flak to be recognized for what it is and discarded. Take, for example, the influence of the first classic demotivator (out of a total of 15):

1. "I just don't feel like it." This catchall demotivator often is accompanied by a yawn or a vague sense of nausea: We get a sinking feeling at the prospect of getting starting with the task at hand. If we press our feelings for more specific information, our internal thoughts might go something like the following. "Do you mean you need more sleep?" No, not exactly. "Do you mean you're ill?" No. "Do you mean that you could do a much better job on the task at some other time?" Probably not.

At this point in our ruminations, we have ferreted out the true content (or lack thereof) of this classic demotivator. If we can locate no good reason why we should procrastinate, we have to consider the unthinkable: actually getting busy. The same kind of interior examination should be undertaken for the rest of the classic demotivators treated here. Our goal in this chapter is to explain the content of the demotivator at hand. Later chapters will deal with how to put these demotivators aside if you determine that they are derailing your true feelings and intentions.

INSIGHT 16 | The general appeal to how we feel is so broad in scope that it can be used to demotivate us for virtually any decision or activity.

Your Turn

Describe some activity or experience you have been putting off because you just don't feel like doing it. Discuss some of the deeper reasons why you might be resisting this activity or experience.

---

2. "I would if I could." This demotivator depicts you as unable to accomplish the task at hand. Again, you must ask yourself whether the de-

motivating statement is true—on at least two levels. First, is it true that you are unable to accomplish the task? If you decide that you have the talent and energy to do the job—as you probably have—go on and ask the second question: Is it true that you would do the task if you decided that you could do it? Here is the sticking point for many of us. We find ourselves admitting that we wouldn't do the task under any circumstances—that we just don't want to do it. We use our supposed inability to do the task as camouflage for the deeper reality that we won't do it in any case.

Once we say that we cannot do something, our additional assurance that we would if we could is often insincere.	**INSIGHT 17**

Your Turn

What do you think people are trying to communicate when they say "I would if I could"? Are they somewhat afraid of the effect of their refusal? What do they hope to gain by using this expression?

3. "It's no use." This classic demotivator asks us to envision outer circumstances so averse to our interests that no amount of effort on our part can make a difference. We need to ask ourselves whether this is an accurate portrayal of the outside world, or whether we are shaping the world to suit (and disguise) our fundamental unwillingness to act. This demotivator does not serve us well if it keeps us from facing up to the real factors influencing our decision whether or not to act.

Giving up at the outset prevents us from exercising creativity and courage to discover how a task might be accomplished.	**INSIGHT 18**

Your Turn

Tell about a time when you initially felt "it's no use" but nevertheless found a way to see a project, activity, or experience through to its conclusion.

4. "It's so difficult!" We all have wilted at one time or another when faced with a large task. This classic demotivator tempts us to envision the total amount of effort necessary to accomplish the entire task, then to decide whether we have that amount of energy on hand at the outset. Often we decide that we're short a volt or two. However, our evaluation might be different if we asked ourselves how much energy it would take simply to begin the task.

INSIGHT 19	The difficulty of a task or activity can be seen as a barrier to action or as a challenge to talent and ability.

Your Turn	
How did you respond the last time you faced a task or activity that you felt was difficult? Did the experience become easier or harder once you began working on it?	

5. "I'm too busy." This demotivator usually involves some exaggeration: It has us look at our busiest day or week and establishes it as typical of our calendar. No wonder we find ourselves too busy to do almost anything in this scenario. A more realistic way to evaluate would be to look at our activity level on an *average* day, not an unusually hectic one, and base judgments on that schedule.

INSIGHT 20	The excuse of scheduling can be used to rule out anything we don't want to do.

Your Turn	
Describe your level of busyness at the present time. What do you wish you could do that you believe you don't have time for?	

6. "I've done that before." The concepts of "new" and "different" are hallmarks of contemporary culture. This demotivator uses this cultural totem to depreciate any activity or task that isn't new or different. For example, we might decide we don't feel like writing a letter to our congres-

sional representative because we've done that before. This demotivator subtly suggests that we aren't moving ahead as we should be so long as we are involved with activities we've done before. Too easily, we can fool ourselves into justifying inactivity on the basis that we don't want to retrace old ground. Fortunately, we do not apply this logic to repetitive activities such as breathing and eating.

Repeating an activity can surprise us with aspects of learning that we did not encounter the first time through.	**INSIGHT 21**

Your Turn

Tell about a repetitive activity that is now part of your school or work life. How do you feel about this activity? How do you deal with the possible boredom that might come with repeating the activity?

7. "Let someone else do it this time." This demotivator, among the subtlest of all, shifts our focus to the supposed lazy, luxuriating "someone" who has so far avoided the workload we have endured. In evaluating whether or not we want to act, we turn our attention not to our own motives or interests but instead to the imagined status of the mythical "someone" who could take our place. Even if we can put a face and name to this someone, we nevertheless fabricate a scenario in which we do too much and the "someone" does far too little. Notice that this demotivator keeps us from confronting the core question of whether we want to do the task—and if not, why not.

Turning a task or responsibility over to "someone" can be a way of rejecting it entirely.	**INSIGHT 22**

Your Turn

Discuss the last time you felt that someone else should be doing a task or activity assigned to you. What did you do? How did things turn out?

8. "What would they say?" Like the previous demotivator, this one creates an "other" or audience that will respond in some devastating way if we undertake a task. What the audience says, of course, is generated not by the audience itself but by our own ventriloquism. We make the audience say what we need to hear in order to justify our inactivity. "Should I take on the chairmanship of the committee? 'They' (the imagined audience) might say that I was too much of a social or organizational climber. I'd better not." In this case, the decision of whether or not to take a leadership role was turned over to an invented chorus of fictional voices. In doing so, the person gives over personal power to others, real or imagined.

INSIGHT 23   The influence of unnamed others is often a projection of our own fears and worries, not an accurate description of the feelings and opinions of those other people.

Your Turn

We all take the opinions and feelings of others into consideration when making some kinds of decisions. Tell about a time when you felt you were influenced by what others would think, feel, or say. How did you deal with your feelings?

---

9. "I'll do it later." In the same way that grass is always greener on the other side of the fence, time is always more available at some later date. By pushing the decision of whether or not to act to some future time, we avoid asking an essential question: What prevents me from acting now? Once I have identified those barriers, how will the passing of time make them go away? Sometimes, of course, we come up with legitimate answers in this kind of inquiry: "Lack of money keeps me from replacing my worn tires this week, but next week I get paid and can afford new tires." That's a legitimate rationale for postponing activity—the passing of time will remove the barrier to action. However, our examination often reveals either that no barriers exist or that the passing of time will not affect them: "I could make a charitable contribution today, but I'll do it later." The barrier in this case is a hidden unwillingness to make the contribution. That unwillingness needs to be addressed, not put off by pushing it into the future.

INSIGHT 24   We are all optimistic enough to think that some future time will be more conducive for work than the present is.

Your Turn

Tell about a task, activity, or experience that you put off for later. Did this delay work as you had intended?

10. "It's not worth it." For any action we take, we no doubt can imagine a best-case result and a worst-case result. This classic demotivator tempts us to imagine only the worst-case result and then to decide not to act at all given the prospect of that worst-case result. For example, children commonly object to cleaning up their toys on the rationale that they will just get strewn around the room again (the worst-case scenario). The prospect that the room will be neat and tidy for a time is not considered. Such worst-scenario thinking can convince a person that virtually any activity is doomed from the beginning and not worth undertaking.

It is difficult at best to measure the outcome or ultimate worth of a task or activity before we even have started it.	**INSIGHT 25**

Your Turn

Tell about a time when you or someone you know used the phrase "it's not worth it." To what were you or they referring? Was the judgment accurate or merely an excuse for inaction?

11. "It's not fair." This demotivator sets up a mental supreme court and calls to the bar the decision of whether or not to act. Let's say, for example, that you are deciding whether it's fair that you should donate your time for the third year in a row as a speaker at a local school. What standards should you apply in deciding the fairness of the situation? The demotivator here calls up the most favorable standards to support inaction. In the ultimate scheme of things, perhaps every other available person should be tapped for speaker duty before you are asked again. However, that appeal to some kind of universal justice takes the focus off more local concerns: Do you want to speak? Fairness, in other words, often can be used as a smokescreen to hide the real issues that are at play in our decision making.

We tend to do what we feel is fair and to resist tasks, duties, and other activities that we believe to be unfair.	**INSIGHT 26**

Your Turn

Describe the last chore, responsibility, or other duty that you felt was assigned to you unfairly. How did you deal with your feelings of unfairness? How did things turn out?

12. "It's not my job." Like some other demotivators, this one directs attention away from what you want toward an imagined document or code that takes decision making out of your hands. One's job, imagined in this way, can expand or contract to accommodate one's deeper and unexamined intentions. This demotivator also includes a forgiveness factor of sorts: No blame apparently can be attached in the case of a decision not to act, because the job supposedly dictated what could or couldn't be done.

INSIGHT 27

People who intend to avoid action and responsibility often do so by narrowly defining their job or required duties.

Your Turn

What do you consider your job description at present? Have you been asked to do a task or activity outside that job description? If so, what? Did you decide to do it?

13. "I wouldn't lift a finger for him!" This demotivator is based on an ad hominem appeal: If I don't like the person, any action associated with that person is equally repugnant to me. Notice that such logic fails entirely when applied to most practical circumstances. If you dislike the president, do you turn down the duties of citizenship? Like most other demotivators, this one has the end result of giving power for decision making to an outside force or person—in this case, an apparent enemy.

INSIGHT 28

Our anger toward others can backfire by preventing us from acting in our own best interests.

Tell about a time when your feelings toward others got in the way of your motivation to perform a task or engage in an activity. What did you learn from the experience?

14. "If I do this, they will expect more." This is the slippery-slope rationale for inaction. In evaluating its core deception, notice that the first half of the proposition ("if I do this") is specific, but the second half ("they will expect more") is entirely open ended. Virtually any negative impact can be included in this second half as a way of discouraging action. Suppose, for example, that a friend has asked you to look over a draft of an important business letter. Using this demotivator, you could talk yourself out of the task by imagining that you will have to proofread all future drafts of the person's entire output of business writing.

Imagining a multiplier effect for any labor you undertake makes almost any activity seem impossibly difficult.   **INSIGHT 29**

Describe a time when your successful performance of one task or responsibility led to requests from others for similar, additional activity on your part. Did you comply?

15. "I don't like working with them." This final demotivator tars the task at hand with the brush of negative feelings for those associated with the task. Suppose you must decide whether to help run a fund-raising effort for an organization to which you belong. You know that the other three people associated with the fund-raiser are not your favorite human beings— one talks too much, another gossips, and the third always seems to be in a bad mood. The core decision of whether or not to assist with the fund-raiser is obscured by the subsidiary matter of working with people you dislike. In effect, you are letting those you dislike prevent you from doing what you might feel you want to do and should do.

Imagining our social relations in advance of experiencing them prevents new and potentially pleasing experiences from interrupting our prejudices.   **INSIGHT 30**

Your Turn

Tell about a time when you initially resisted a task or activity because of the people involved. How did things turn out? What did you learn?

Summing Up

The human penchant for resisting new experiences and avoiding work has generated a wide array of classic demotivators. Examined closely, each of these excuses contains components that war against our best interests. Learning to recognize the influence of classic demotivators is the first step in resisting them.

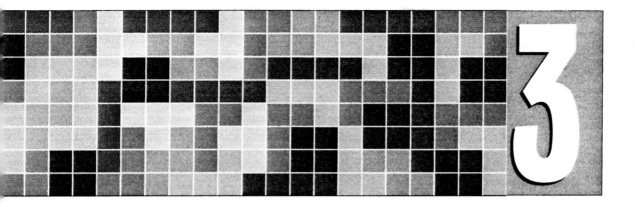

Assessing Your Primary Motivators

GOALS

- Understand that the choice of personal motivators depends on our individual tendencies and experiences.

- Measure our selection of primary motivators.

- Interpret the meaning of those selections.

In the following assessment, you will discover valuable insights into your mental habits with regard to motivation. Telling you about these mental habits in advance of the test would skew its results. Therefore, approach these questions with an open mind and give candid answers. There are no right or wrong responses. Your answers simply will indicate certain tendencies on your part with regard to motivation. Knowing what these tendencies are gives you a chance not only to make the most of them, but also to prevent a tendency from allowing you to make other, perhaps better choices at times.

Exercise 1

Directions: Read each question carefully. Select the answer that matches your feelings. (In some cases, neither answer will fit your feelings precisely. In those cases, choose the answer that comes closer than the other answer to your feelings.) When you have completed the assessment, transfer your answers to the answer sheet at the end of the test. There you also will find an interpretation of your scores.

1. You have a major examination coming up as part of your college study or work life. Which would be more effective in motivating you to study?
   a. encouragement from my professor or boss
   b. my ambition

2. A new job has opened up in your company. You are deciding whether or not to apply for it. Which would be more effective in motivating you to apply?
   a. information from the company assuring you that all applicants will have a fair chance
   b. your own ideas about where this new job could lead you on your upward career path

3. You are trying to decide whether to rent an attractive apartment at a rental rate that is significantly higher than you are now paying. Which would be more effective in motivating you to rent the apartment?
   a. your confidence in yourself and your financial future
   b. moral support from friends and relatives who would like to see you living in a nicer place

4. You are working on a project along with four other people. A looming deadline requires that you work on a Saturday without additional compensation. Which would be more effective in motivating you to work on the Saturday?
   a. your idea that the boss will take note of this extra effort and reward you in some way in the future
   b. the fact that the other four people on the project have agreed to work on Saturday

5. You are contemplating a change in careers. Which would be more effective in motivating you to make the change?
   a. advice from those who know you and your abilities best, including a favorite college professor
   b. your belief that a career change would make work more interesting and rewarding for you

(continued)

6. Three people in your work group received a raise this year and three did not. You were one of the ones who did not. You are deciding whether or not to talk with your boss about this situation. Which would be more effective in motivating you to talk with your boss?
   a. the rumor that your performance appraisal was just as good as those of the people who received the raise
   b. your idea that making the boss aware of your negative feelings about the situation will encourage him to give you a raise sooner rather than later

7. Your company sports team wants you to join. You do not feel that you are a particularly good player. Which would be more effective in motivating you to join the team?
   a. your willingness to accept new challenges and try new experiences
   b. friendly invitations and encouragement from several members of the team who really want you to join

8. You are shopping for a new car. The salesperson has stated a price and you are deciding whether or not to buy. Which would be more effective in motivating you to buy the car?
   a. your expectation that you could not find the car cheaper elsewhere
   b. your knowledge that two of your friends bought the same car model for the same price within the last few weeks

9. Your boss tells you that you have been asked to be a speaker for the company at an upcoming convention. Which would be more effective in motivating you to accept this speaking invitation?
   a. your boss's statement that you would be making a big contribution to the company as a speaker
   b. your confidence that you could represent the company well as a speaker

10. Economic conditions have forced your company to consider pay cutbacks for all workers. Which would be more effective in motivating you to accept the pay cut?
    a. the knowledge that all workers are receiving the same percentage of cut in their pay
    b. your belief that your company will appreciate your willingness to accept a pay cut and will reward you when better times return

11. You are trying to decide where to go on vacation. Which would be more effective in motivating you to select a particular location?
    a. your long-term desire to see that part of the world
    b. reports from friends who have returned recently from that region

(*continued*)

Exercise 1   (continued)

12. One of your friends complains to you that she isn't getting ahead in her job as quickly as she would like. Which of these approaches would you use in motivating her to talk to her employer about the problem?
    a. You urge her to assemble proof that other workers in her group with less skill and experience have been moved ahead more quickly than she has.
    b. You urge her to put together work materials showing how valuable she can be to the company in a more advanced position.

13. Due to circumstances beyond your control, you have to turn in a term paper late. You are worried that the professor will not accept the paper. Which would be more effective in motivating you to talk with the professor about the problem?
    a. advice from another classmate who had the same professor last semester
    b. your belief that the professor will be reasonable in understanding the circumstances

14. Parking spots are hard to find at your workplace. An assigned parking place close to the building is highly prized. You have waited for such a spot for more than 2 years. However, when a prime parking spot became available, it was given to an employee who had not been with the company as long as you had. You are deciding whether or not to complain to senior management. Which would be more effective in motivating you to complain about the problem?
    a. the lack of fairness involved in passing you over for a more junior employee
    b. the influence this slight will have on your morale and productivity in the company in the future

15. You are deciding whether to join a community college class to learn a foreign language. Which would be more effective in motivating you to join the class?
    a. your desire to learn the language
    b. the fact that two of your friends are already in the class and like it very much

16. You have just graduated from college and have no particular job prospects. Which would be more effective in motivating you to search the job ads in the newspaper?
    a. your hope of finding a position that interests you
    b. your idea that not finding a position would be a waste of the effort and expense you put into college

17. You are trying to read in a library. Two librarians are talking loudly a short distance from you. Which would be more effective in motivating you to ask the librarians to talk more quietly?
    a. the sign posted near the library door: "Please maintain QUIET in the library."
    b. your growing irritation at being unable to concentrate on your reading due to the librarians' chatter

(continued)	**Exercise 1**

18. Your elderly parents are drawing up their wills, with financial provisions for you and your younger brother. Your parents ask you in private whether you would like to inherit their life insurance (a fixed amount) or their stocks, which could rise or fall in value in the period prior to their deaths. What motivates you to select the stocks?
    a. If you do receive substantially more than your brother (who will receive the life insurance), you can point out that you took the risk that the stocks could have gone down.
    b. The stocks have a chance of becoming much more valuable than they are at present.

19. You must decide whether to spend money for new clothes for an upcoming business trip. Which is more effective in motivating your decision?
    a. It's been a while since you bought new clothes and you feel you deserve them.
    b. Several work associates who will accompany you on the trip already have told you about their plans to buy new clothes.

20. Contrary to the usual policy of allowing managers to use company cars for entertaining clients, the new policy prohibits the use of company cars in this way for all employees below the vice-president level. You are not yet a vice president. Which would you be motivated to do?
    a. accept the new policy without complaint because you hope you will soon be named a vice president in the company
    b. accept the new policy without complaint because it applies equally to everyone at your level in the organization

21. A good friend has recently lost her job. Which approach would you tend to use in encouraging the friend to seek another job?
    a. gather help-wanted ads that might be suitable for your friend
    b. tell your friend how valuable her talents are

22. Membership at the company gym is determined by drawing, because many more employees sought membership than the gym could accommodate. Which would be more effective in motivating you to enter your name in the drawing?
    a. the idea that all employees have the same chance, assuming the drawing is fair
    b. your expectation that you might get lucky and be drawn as a new gym member

23. The grass around your home desperately needs to be mowed. Which would be more effective in motivating you to do the job yourself?
    a. You know you have the strength and equipment to do the job.
    b. You have seen many of your neighbors mowing their own grass.

(continued)

Exercise 1   (continued)

24. At the circus, you are deciding whether to pay a dollar for a chance to knock down three milk bottles with a softball and win a prize. You end up deciding not to do so. Which is more effective in determining your decision?
    a. You aren't sure you throw a softball well enough to hit the bottles.
    b. You suspect that the milk bottles have been weighted so that they won't fall down easily.

25. You have the opportunity to buy stock in a promising new company. Which would be more effective in determining your decision?
    a. the optimistic attitudes of two of your friends who also are investing in the company
    b. your ability to take reasonable risks, for better or for worse

26. You have tickets to attend the theater. However, you are disappointed when a famous actor scheduled to play the lead role fails to show up. His understudy takes over and the show goes on. Which is the main source of your disappointment?
    a. On other evenings, theatergoers paid the same price for tickets and saw the famous actor, not the understudy.
    b. You had looked forward to seeing the famous actor perform.

27. You are trying to decide whether or not to return to college to earn an additional degree. Which would be more effective in motivating you to do so?
    a. your desire to learn more and confidence in your abilities
    b. stories from your friends about how much they enjoyed returning to college

28. You have worked hard and well for the company for more than a year—but so far without a raise. Which would be more likely to motivate you to expect a raise in the near future?
    a. The boss knows you have been expecting a raise and aren't willing to wait much longer without quitting
    b. The company has a history of rewarding good performance sooner or later

29. You are shopping for a ring. Which would be more effective in motivating you to buy one?
    a. the jeweler's assurance that you are buying a quality ring at a deeply discounted price
    b. your own good shopping sense if you find the right ring

30. After 5 years with the company, you and nine other workers each receive a small pin at a luncheon in your honor. Which would be your more likely reaction?
    a. satisfaction, because all workers who had worked at the company for 5 years received the same pin
    b. dissatisfaction, because you were an outstanding worker and you expected the company to present you with something more substantial than a pin after 5 years

| **(continued)** | **Exercise 1** |

Scoring

Place checks for your "a" or "b" choices in these columns:

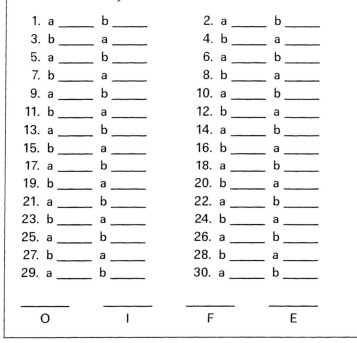

1. a _____ b _____	2. a _____ b _____
3. b _____ a _____	4. b _____ a _____
5. a _____ b _____	6. a _____ b _____
7. b _____ a _____	8. b _____ a _____
9. a _____ b _____	10. a _____ b _____
11. b _____ a _____	12. b _____ a _____
13. a _____ b _____	14. a _____ b _____
15. b _____ a _____	16. b _____ a _____
17. a _____ b _____	18. a _____ b _____
19. b _____ a _____	20. b _____ a _____
21. a _____ b _____	22. a _____ b _____
23. b _____ a _____	24. b _____ a _____
25. a _____ b _____	26. a _____ b _____
27. b _____ a _____	28. b _____ a _____
29. a _____ b _____	30. a _____ b _____

```
  _____    _____          _____    _____
     O          I                F          E
```

INTERPRETATION

The higher your score is in any column, the more dominant that tendency is in your approach to self-motivation.

O—Outside motivators. If your score is higher in the "O" column than in the "I" column, you tend to pay more attention to what others say and feel as a motivational influence. On the positive side, your knowledge of this tendency can make you aware of the advice, comments, feedback, and guidance provided by others. You tend, after all, to find this information crucial to your motivation and decision making. Knowing it accurately and extensively can help you find powerful motivators. On the other hand, you might want to guard against too complete a reliance on the opinions of others to the exclusion of knowing your own mind and heart. A high tendency score in this column also could be your warning to think hard about what *you* think, want, feel, and need.

I—Inside motivators. If your score is higher in the "I" column than in the "O" column, you tend to find your motivation more in your own thoughts and feelings than in what others think and feel. Your high score can indicate the positive influence of knowing who you are and what you want. You are able on most occasions to shut out the distracting and conflicting opinions and advice of the outside world so that you can hear your own authentic intentions and perspective. On the other hand, a tendency to shut out the world can be hazardous if practiced too rigidly. A high score in this column might alert you to a tendency to discount all opinions other than your own. You might want to listen not only to your own inner voice but also to the outside voices that you respect.

F—Fairness. If your score is higher in the "F" column than in the "E" column, you tend to be motivated more by a sense of fairness than by your expectation for what might occur. A high score in this column indicates that you are "moved" (i.e., motivated) by equity in human affairs. When you feel you or someone else has been treated unjustly, you are energized to action. In the great scheme of things, this sensitivity to fairness is no doubt admirable. However, if you focus only on fairness in a notoriously unfair world, you might find yourself enmeshed in endless efforts to make things right instead of making things move forward. For example, your aversion to instances of unfairness in a large corporation could involve all your energies in an effort to correct the situation. Although such a crusade is undoubtedly noble, it often might take the place of other worthwhile career goals you could be pursuing.

E—Expectation. If your score is higher in the "E" column than in the "F" column, you tend to be motivated more by what you expect or hope will happen rather than by what you feel is fair or deserved. A high score in this column indicates that you tend to be motivated by "blue sky"—that is, the endless possibilities of the future. This optimism for what lies ahead is a wonderful quality, and your friends probably admire it in you. The downside of motivation by expectancy, however, is that many of our fondest dreams for tomorrow never materialize. That reality can leave us embittered or, just as often, ceaselessly chasing pots of gold at the end of rainbows invisible to all but ourselves. If your score is high in this column, you might want to reflect on the value of tempering expectation-based motivation with other, more immediate goals and rewards.

Summing Up

In selecting among alternative motivators, we reveal our tendencies and personality. Such choices are neither right or wrong, but they can prove useful or useless in varying circumstances. Knowing what we tend to favor as a motivator gives us the opportunity to investigate other motivational options beyond those habitual choices.

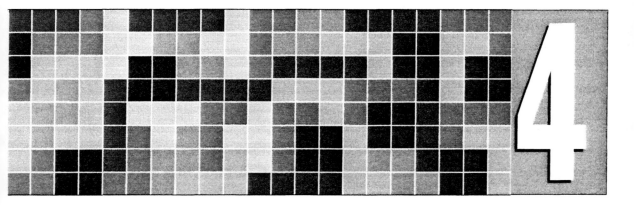

Motivation from the Inside

GOALS

- Recognize the deep personal roots of our prime motivators.
- Understand and use to our advantage the hierarchy of motivational influence.
- Grasp the motivating influence of culture and religion on some of our most important decisions.

Many of our most powerful motivators do not come from the outside world—what others urge us to do—but instead from the inner world of our individual consciousness (and subconsciousness), memories, experiences, and personality predispositions. These inner motivations gain their power in part because we feel they spring from our own will and power of self-direction. We usually don't argue with our own impulses to the same degree that we might resist outside prompts, orders, and pressures.

SILENT MOTIVATORS AND RATIONAL MOTIVATORS

This chapter will deal with silent motivators—those felt or sensed—as well as verbal motivators—those we think about rationally in some form of language. To make the distinction between these categories clear, imagine yourself in front of the television watching your favorite show. Silent motivators on this occasion might include a nagging urge to make some popcorn, a need to shift in your chair or on the couch for comfort, and perhaps a need to use the rest room during the commercial. Although these motivators are highly effective in causing you to act, none of them announce themselves as voices that you hear within. Your yen for popcorn does not come to you as a language string—"you are growing hungry for popcorn." Instead, it is expressed as vague feelings in the mouth, stomach, and elsewhere. From these motivating feelings comes your decision to satisfy your hunger (that is, respond to silent motivators) by making popcorn. As you eat the popcorn, similar motivators might send you back to the kitchen for a drink of some kind.

INSIGHT 31	Motivational influence is often nonverbal.

Your Turn	

What silent motivators are influencing you at this moment? How will they affect your actions in the next few hours?

Rational motivators, by contrast, are characterized by our conscious attention to ideas, images, impressions, and language fragments within. The term 'rational' in this case does not suggest that these motivators are logical, although they might be. In the case of rational motivators, we engage our thinking ('rational') powers. Take the following example of a rational motivator. While watching a television show, you view a commercial that urges you to phone an 800 number to purchase exercise equipment ("three easy payments of $49.95"). Your inner motivation to do so is not silent, as in the case of hunger. Instead, you mull over bits and pieces of thoughts, feelings, images, impressions, and memories in determining whether to pick up the phone.

Except in certain forms of mental illness such as schizophrenia, these inner thoughts usually do not express themselves to us as voices speaking fully formed messages. You probably do not hear a distinct voice inside saying "Lose 10 pounds and look great in your clothes by purchasing exercise equipment now." Your experience of inner motivation is much more diffuse and abstract. You might think about being overweight or out of shape, but you hardly form complete sentences as you weigh whether to make the call. Your conscious thinking processes certainly are engaged, but your inner experience of self-debate takes place in a highly abbreviated language, a kind of mental shorthand. Fragments of ideas and words occur only to be quickly replaced by other, often contradictory half-thoughts and impressions. Out of this jumble, you decide whether your motivation to call is stronger than your motivation not to call. Even after you have made your decision, the inner debate might continue (in a process called "second-guessing ourselves"). By then, of course, you have forgotten the phone number.

We experience many motivators in fragmentary form, mixing interior language, impressions, ideas, and feelings.   **INSIGHT 32**

Your Turn

Make an effort to describe one of the main ways in which you experience motivation. Does such influence come to you as a complete, sentence-like thought? If not, describe the experience of this motivation as accurately as you can.

BASIC PHYSICAL MOTIVATORS

Central to the investigation of silent motivators has been Abraham Maslow's hypothesis that within each of us dwells a hierarchy of needs, symbolically expressed as a layered pyramid as shown on the next page.

It was Maslow's insight in *Motivation and Personality* (2nd ed., 1970) that we human beings do not select inner motivators randomly or whimsically, but instead follow a system of priorities (or *needs*, according to Maslow) in making our selection. Significantly, silent motivators form the base of the motivation pyramid and demand first priority when competing with other possible motivators.

Maslow called this foundation level of the motivation pyramid our "physiological needs." He has in mind our powerful motive to breathe, eat, sleep, void, and express sexual impulses. Once these motivators are attended to, humans are free to be influenced by levels of motivation that are higher on the pyramid. The key point for our purposes is this: Until foundation-level motivators are dealt with, other forms of motivation will have little influence on us.

You have no doubt experienced this competition between foundation-level and higher-level motivators. Recall a time when you sat in a class or meeting where the room temperature was much too warm or too cold. Your

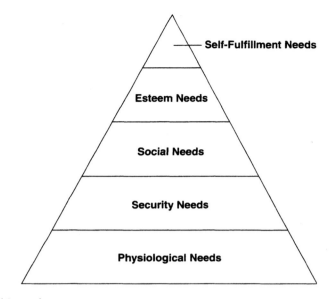

Maslow's hierarchy.

Source: From *Motivation and Personality*, 3rd ed. by Abraham Maslow. Revised by Robert Frager et al. Copyright © 1954, 1987 by Harper & Row Publishers, Inc. Copyright © Abraham H. Maslow. Reprinted by permission of Addison-Wesley Educational Publishers, Inc.

physiological motive to seek comfort probably occupied much of your attention and energy. You might have found yourself unable to concentrate on what the professor or meeting leader was saying (a higher-level motive) simply because your foundation-level motivators had not been dealt with.

Maslow did not suggest that the dominance of foundation-level motivators was absolute. Gandhi's experience with levels of motivation is a case in point. During his famous hunger strikes, he was able to look past his need for food to other, higher motivators. Maslow does argue that as a general rule, human beings find it difficult to attend to higher-level motivators until foundation-level needs have been satisfied.

At least two lessons grow out of Maslow's insights into the physiological level of motivators:

- When you find yourself unable to decide what you want (in effect, prioritize your motivators), take a moment to consider whether your physiological needs are at a reasonable level of comfort.
- In preparation for involvement in an activity, resolve any physiological motivators before attempting to attend to higher-level motivators.

INSIGHT 33   Our basic physiological needs exert dominant motivational influence.

Tell about a time when a physiological motivator kept you from attending to other, 'higher-level' motivators. How did things turn out?

At the next level in Maslow's hierarchy are security needs. At this level, we are motivated in part by physical motives (for example, to shelter ourselves from the cold) and psychological motives (for example, to rest comfortably in a safe place).

You might have experienced the conflict between security needs and higher-level motives in college or in the workplace. A bomb scare, for example, can derail student or employee productivity for hours if not days. Thinking about a disastrous explosion in the building (a threat to our need for security) keeps us from attending to other, higher-level motives, such as our desire to perform well on an examination or a company project. We use expressions such as "my mind is just not on my work" to explain the conflict we feel between levels of motivation.

A second example involves job insecurity. Imagine that your ability to pay your rent or mortgage, put food on the table, and pay your monthly bills depends entirely on receiving your usual paycheck. Now think about how you would feel if your company announced that it would be terminating half of its employees in the next 2 months due to financial problems. Even before you find out if you will lose your job, the motive to care about your security probably overrides all other motives at work. It becomes almost impossible to give your best to company tasks when the prospect of being fired (and, by extension, being unable to meet your monthly expenses) looms over your head.

The lesson here is straightforward: At times when you are fearful about basic security issues, you probably cannot expect yourself to give full or even adequate attention to other motivators. The term *fearful* in this case does not necessarily mean an extreme state of anxiety. Even vague uneasiness occasioned by security concerns can act to cancel the influence of other motivators.

Worries about security and our motivation to achieve security usually take priority over the motivators higher on Maslow's hierarchy.   **INSIGHT 34**

Tell about a time when you felt that your security was threatened in some way. How did you eventually get your mind back to other matters?

PSYCHOLOGICAL AND SOCIAL MOTIVATORS

The remaining layers in Maslow's hierarchy depict motivators that have their source in social and psychological needs. These are the levels of social needs, esteem needs, and self-fulfillment needs. Although the names are self-explanatory, an example of each might help clarify Maslow's hypotheses.

At the level of social needs, we are each motivated to a greater or lesser degree to seek friendships, camaraderie, and a sense of belonging. Even those who consider themselves to be somewhat shy or loners feel the motivation in some circumstances to join in conversation or become a member of a group or team.

INSIGHT 35

We all have social needs to one degree or another; these needs act as strong motivators in our selection of tasks and activities.

Your Turn

Describe a time when you were influenced to act in a certain way by a social group. How did the group exert its influence?

When social needs have been addressed, Maslow argues, we can turn more attentively to motivators having to do with our esteem needs. At this layer on the hierarchy pyramid, we aren't content simply to share membership in a group. We desire a certain degree of respect, attention, admiration, and perhaps even love from the most significant people in our lives. Acting on these motivators, we might run for office; seek promotions at work; publicize ourselves and our interests, perhaps by a personal Web site or other means; and seek out the company of those who give us compliments and other forms of regard.

When we have satisfied motivators related to personal esteem, we graduate as it were to Maslow's highest level of need or motivation: self-fulfillment. At this level, we attend to motivators that have to do with our sense of personal destiny, life plan, or ultimate ambition. We also are motivated to let our various talents flourish, perhaps by pursuing music lessons, joining an athletic team, or taking on an intellectual project or avocation of some kind.

INSIGHT 36

Esteem and self-fulfillment motivators usually can express themselves only after lower-level needs have been resolved.

Discuss motivators that are leading you to self-fulfillment. What are you trying to achieve? What motivates you to do so?

THE PEOPLE BEHIND THE MOTIVATORS

Viewed from the internal perspective of an individual, the motivators found at these levels stem largely from experiences, pro and con, with significant individuals in our past. Among these influential people are the following.

Parents. Certainly since Freud, several generations of psychiatrists, psychologists, and other therapists and counselors have spent much of their energy in one endeavor: helping patients recognize and deal with the pervasive psychological influence of their parents throughout adult life.

Here's a simple test to locate the background presence of Mom or Dad (or grandparent, influential sibling, and so on) in a given motivator. When you feel or call to mind the motivator (for example, "I really should get to bed before 11 P.M."), ask the question, "Why?" As thoughts filter through your mind in answer to that question, listen especially for memories or "scripts" from your upbringing. Using this approach, we often discover that some of our most powerful motivators have more to do with pleasing our parents (even after they are deceased) than with following our own wills. When this confusion between what parents seem to want and what the individual wants becomes fraught with tension and pain, mental health professionals attempt to step in to help untangle the mixed messages and motives felt by the individual.

At a more common level, we each can go far toward understanding the sources of some of our motivators by separating what Mom or Dad would have wanted from what we as adults want on our own behalf. Particularly if we are plagued with an excess of "should" motivators ("I should work harder," "I should visit my aunt more often," "I should avoid stress," and so forth), there can be genuine relief in accurately identifying those "shoulds" not with our own authentic wishes but instead with the echoing influence of parental memories we carry within.

One of our most potent motivators is the influence of our parents, especially as we internalize that influence and identify it as our feelings instead of our parents'.

INSIGHT 37

Your Turn

Describe some form of motivation that you realize comes from your parents. How do you feel about their motivational influence in your life?

Mentors, teachers, and admired individuals. In addition to parents, we each carry with us the influence of many other individuals for whom we had (or have) emotional bonds of respect, esteem, or love. These men and women often play the role of models for us in various areas of endeavor. We might cling to memories of one person as the ideal boss and of another as the near-perfect friend or confidant. It stands to reason that when we must choose our own path as boss, friend, or confidant, we think back to these memorable people from our past and attempt to emulate their qualities and actions.

On balance, the motivation to imitate "best practices" is a healthy and progressive use of the past. It backfires only when we place admired people on such elevated pedestals that we judge ourselves to be perpetual failures in their shadows.

In interpreting motivators that stem from mentors, teachers, and admired individuals, we can save ourselves considerable anxiety by not overrating their expectations of us ("He would roll over in his grave if he saw me now"), making unproductive comparisons ("I'll never be the manager she was!"), and inflating events or reputations ("He never lost his temper"). Being realistic about those we admire helps us attend to motivators within the realm of possibility rather than grandiose ambitions that come to nothing.

INSIGHT 38   Living up to the imagined expectations of those we admire exerts a powerful motivational effect.

Your Turn

Describe a mentor, teacher, or admired individual who has motivated you in some way. What was or is the nature of that motivation?

Friends and significant others. We also carry around within us the motivational influence of past and present friendships. Particularly when it comes to decisions about relationships and social matters, we might view new situations through the filters of past experiences. These filters often exert a veto power—

in effect, a negative motivation—over actions we are contemplating: "I'll never date a doctoral student again," "I never enjoy parties where I don't know most of the people," "I can only trust a friend who doesn't have too many other close friends," and so forth. These judgments frequently stem from old, perhaps traumatic experiences with previous friends and relationships.

For all their positive influence, friends as carried in memory can exert a stranglehold on our development—and fun—as individuals. Past experiences do not predict accurately what we will encounter in the future. Detaching automatic responses based on the past from our motivation for social involvement can open the door to delight.

We often are moved to act out of regard for those we like or love.	**INSIGHT 39**

Your Turn

Tell about a recent occasion in which the influence of friends or significant others proved to be a strong motivating influence on you.

SOURCES OF PERSONAL MOTIVATION IN CULTURE AND RELIGION

Many of our most powerful recurring motivators stem from sources beyond parents, mentors, and friends. Here is a sampler of such motivators.

Cultural Motivators

- "As a Native American, I am motivated to explore myths and legends important to my ancestors."
- "My Scandinavian roots have led me to a lifelong interest in early explorers."
- "I'm motivated to study Italian because my grandparents came from Italy and I'm visiting there next summer."

In these cases, notice that membership in a culture can promote motivation but does not create it automatically. For instance, many Scandinavians aren't interested in early explorers, and many Italian Americans never learn to speak Italian. Cultural motivators are best viewed as a fertile ground from which predispositions and passions might emerge. We each can turn to the culture(s) to which we belong to see what can grow with a bit of nurturing.

INSIGHT 40	Cultural influences, as motivators, do not force us to make specific choices; instead, they offer options for social involvement beyond the limits of our usual group.

Your Turn	

Choose one cultural influence that affects you as a motivator. Where did that cultural influence come from? How do you feel about it?

Religious Motivators

- "I donate time to feeding the homeless because I believe God's love is intended to flow through people."
- "I am motivated to meditate because, as a Buddhist, I believe I can attain higher consciousness through this means."
- "My memories of Sunday school as a child motivate me to make sure my own children attend Sunday school regularly."

Like cultural motivators, religious stimuli to action can be powerfully felt and deeply influence our actions. In most major religions, in fact, spiritual stories and lessons have the explicit purpose of motivating changes in the attitudes and behaviors of believers.

INSIGHT 41	Like culture, religious belief presents motivational opportunities for changes in thoughts, feelings, and actions.

Your Turn	

Describe the influence of religion as a motivator on someone you know well (perhaps yourself).

WHAT YOU EXPECT OF YOURSELF

So far in this chapter, we have focused on the influence of ghosts, as it were—parents, mentors, friends, and others—who might be the partial or entire source of some of your prime motivators. However, you are not simply a collection of other people's perspectives. As Carl Jung proposed in his famous theory of personality types, we bring some of our main personality tendencies with us from earliest childhood, perhaps even from birth. The motivators we find most influential, understandably, are linked closely to those personality tendencies.

Jung's theories and their applications are explored in depth in *Developing Leadership Abilities* in this series. For our purposes here, it is enough to point out the eight major bases of personality in Jung's view. From this array of personality types, you probably will be able to spot your own personality type. After locating that type, you can consider practical ways to apply your knowledge of personality to the art of personal motivation.

In finding your approximate personality category, recognize that you might have more than one dominant tendency in your personality. For example, a Feeler also might have strong Member qualities. A Thinker, by contrast, often has the qualities of the Self and the Researcher.

Planner. This personality type values schedules, projections, time lines, outlines, and organization in all its forms. The Planner feels uncomfortable in the presence of unexpected or unusual developments and might be less than successful in coping with crisis and change.

Juggler. This personality type enjoys the stimulation of having "many balls in the air." The Juggler takes pride in being able to provide at least minimal management oversight for a multitude of projects at the same time. The Juggler becomes bored quickly in a static, routine environment. Emergencies are viewed by the Juggler as a chance to rise to the occasion as a jack of all trades.

The Planner and Juggler personality types are polar opposites, each with its own typical motivators and preferences.	**INSIGHT 42**

Your Turn
Decide whether you are closer to a Planner or a Juggler in your attitudes and life habits. What motivators within you appear to go along with your identification with either the Planner or Juggler type?

Researcher. This personality type attempts to pursue information until feeling highly confident in its accuracy. The Researcher is naturally curious and might dispense with big-picture thinking to chase down an apparently trivial question or missing bit of data. The Researcher resists easy answers, consensus judgments not supported by thorough evidence, and any rush to judgment.

Closer. This personality type views time as money and wants to save both. The Closer wants to bring resolution to matters of debate or negotiation. The Closer will be among the first in a group to suggest that a vote be taken to determine the outcome of an issue. This personality type is uncomfortable in an environment characterized by free discussion, far-ranging speculation, and full participation by discussants.

INSIGHT 43	The Researcher and Closer personality types are polar opposites, each with its own typical motivators and preferences.

Your Turn	
Do you feel yourself to be more a Researcher or a Closer? Why?	

Feeler. This personality type evaluates the worth of any action or idea on how it impacts the emotions of the group. The Feeler favors activities that encourage group morale and resists activities that pit group members against one another in an aggressive way. The Feeler stays in close touch with each group member and usually is known as a good listener. The Feeler might be ineffective when unpopular decisions must be made.

Thinker. This personality type values logic, rationality, and orderly decision-making processes. The Thinker might overlook or undervalue emotional or political considerations in coming to important decisions. The Thinker often is viewed as an outsider or subversive by group members, but at the same time this personality type is valued for its intellectual contributions.

INSIGHT 44	The Feeler and Thinker personality types are polar opposites, each with its own typical motivators and preferences.

Your Turn	
Consider whether you are more a Feeler or a Thinker. List several personal motivators that lead you to believe you are closer to one of these personality types than the other.	

Member. This personality type seeks social relationships for security, validation of personal worth, and enjoyable interaction. The Member resists making decisions or taking action before consultation with and support from the group. The Member interprets participation in the group as a sign of one's individual worth and popularity.

Self. This personality type prefers solitary reflection to group interaction. The Self resists membership in groups where independence of perspective and judgment is hindered. The Self finds experiences fulfilling when they meet the Self's individual standards, not when they are approved by a group. The Self is a loner whose interests might appear selfish when measured against the interests of group members.

The Member and Self personality types are polar opposites, each with its own typical motivators and preferences.	**INSIGHT 45**

	Your Turn
Are you by nature a Member or a Self? Name a few personal motivators that support your choice.	

Have you located your central personality tendencies? If so, here's how to leverage that knowledge into a useful way of generating and interpreting personal motivators. Begin by listing the motivators that seem to fit with your dominant personality traits. For example, if you determine that you are by nature a Planner, you might find that such motivators as the following are familiar to you:

- I like to plan my schedule of activities at least one day in advance.
- I tend to get along best with people who are orderly, careful, and organized.
- I am most motivated to participate in activities and projects in which my planning skills are needed and valued.

So much for the familiar. In this way, you have assembled several motivators that fit naturally with your personality tendencies. However, for the sake of reaching your full potential, you also will want to examine motivators that get overridden by your strong Planner tendencies (or whatever the traits are of your dominant type). These are the motivators that usually contain the word *but*:

- I like to try new things, *but* I quickly lose interest if activities aren't well organized.
- I am motivated to pitch in during crisis and change, *but* it annoys me when other people can't see the importance of good planning.
- I enjoy meeting all kinds of people, *but* I get along best with those who have their act together in terms of personal scheduling and an organized approach to life.

The "buts" in these statements should be interpreted as a caution. Although your motivators might be leading you in new and interesting directions, your core personality tendencies could be holding you back. Use your knowledge of personality type, therefore, not only to spot (and seek out) expected motivators in harmony with that personality type, but also to avoid your own motivation censorship as new possibilities conflict with established personality traits.

INSIGHT 46   Knowing our main personality tendencies does not mean that we must be bound by them.

Your Turn

Tell about a time when you consciously acted in a way that was not typical for your basic personality tendencies. How did you feel? What did you learn?

Summing Up

We carry within us conscious and unconscious influences from our genetic makeup, life experiences, influences from other people, cultural and religious backgrounds, and many other voices. Getting to know these main sources of motivation gives us a chance not only to evaluate their influence and activity in our lives, but also to go beyond them purposely to prevent being imprisoned by our pasts.

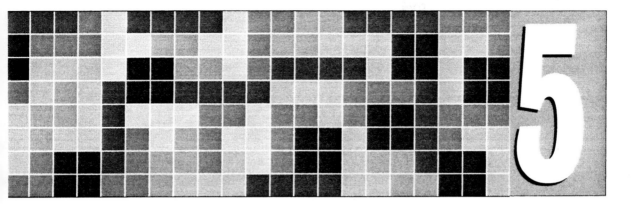

Motivation from the Outside

GOALS

- Identify the major external sources of motivators that influence our decision making.
- Learn to evaluate and control the power of those external influences.
- Distinguish between what others want us to do and what we ourselves want to do.

So far we have discussed motivators stemming from internal sources, whether physical, psychological, cultural, or religious. As we have seen, these sources often harken back to your basic personality disposition or the values and life habits of parents, friends, mentors, and others. These voices become part of you and emerge (often in disguised form) as motivators, often telling you what you should or shouldn't do.

We move on now to motivators stemming from external sources. These voices are not disguised or shadowy at all. They are the oral and written, verbal and nonverbal messages sent to you by all the agenda makers in your life: bosses, professors, organization leaders, politicians, religious leaders, and many others. This chapter shows you how to receive these attempts at motivation in a nondefensive, evaluative way. In addition, the chapter will show what to do if orders without accompanying motivators come to you from authority figures. If you are tired of people "pushing your buttons," you probably will find value here in learning what those buttons are; how people attempt to push them against your wishes; and how you can determine how, when, and why you respond to motivators from external sources.

INSIGHT 47	Authority figures can be viewed as would-be agenda makers for our day-to-day life experiences.

Your Turn	
Describe one authority figure who now exerts strong influence in your daily life. How do you feel about this authority figure?	

MOTIVATORS FROM LIFE'S TASKMASTERS

From preschool days onward, we spend most of our waking hours in the presence of culturally supported taskmasters. These are the many men and women who have a license to tell us what to do. That license can come in the form of a teaching credential, a position of authority as a boss, election or appointment to a leadership position in government, or some other mode. After some initial kicking and screaming as tots, we tend to give in to these taskmasters and (with some grousing) do what they tell us.

Notice three interesting aspects of our relationship with life's taskmasters:

1. The power of motivators from the taskmaster comes from the taskmaster's position of authority, not from the intrinsic persuasiveness of the motivator itself.

Only a small portion of the motivators we receive from taskmasters are couched in attractive terms that appeal to our interests and personalities. We quickly grow used to accepting motivation as the exercise of power over us, not the influence of persuasion. For example, most of the assignments we completed in school at whatever level were given on the basis of authority. If a professor said a test would be given in the class, we usually accepted that fact without question. If the boss required a certain dress code at work, we probably complied. After a steady diet of receiving and following orders, some people begin to seek out environments where they are told what to do. In these environments, as the saying goes, "the slave creates the master." Those who do not live comfortably in an environment of constant orders from an authority figure might become demoralized and cynical. Even if they obey orders, they do so halfheartedly, all the while despising the order giver.

Taskmasters attempt to motivate us by the exercise of power.	**INSIGHT 48**

Your Turn

Describe in specific terms the power that a particular taskmaster has over you at present. How is that power exercised? What would happen if you resisted it by making different choices than those intended by the taskmaster?

2. An order from a taskmaster is not necessarily a motivator. We can make orders more palatable and motivating by discovering their intent.

When your boss gives you a task to do, your motivation to undertake the job might be low indeed. One way to increase your motivation to complete the task is to discover unspoken motivators that lie behind the boss's order.

Consider this scenario, for example. Richard, a relatively new employee in the customer service division of a major department store, receives a direct order from his boss not to use the phrase "I'm sorry" in talking with customers about their complaints. Richard finds this order strange, to say the least. He reasons that he should apologize when the store has failed to satisfy the customer in some way. Instead of blindly following the order, Richard engages his boss in a friendly (not defensive) conversation:

Richard: "I would like to learn more about your thinking about using the words 'I'm sorry' with customers."

Boss: "I'm glad you asked. The legal department has asked us to resolve customer complaints without verbally admitting liability. It does feel awkward not to apologize in some circumstances. But usually you can simply move ahead with the customer to the resolution of the problem."

In this case, Richard has broadened his knowledge of company culture and now has a rationale for following the boss's order. Lacking that rationale, Richard would come over time to feel more and more like a pawn among the company players—someone expected to park his brains at the door before entering the workplace.

INSIGHT 49	Blindly accepting the orders, agendas, and directions of taskmasters leaves us relatively helpless to escape their influence eventually.

Your Turn	

Discuss a time when you sought out and found the rationale that lay behind an order given to you by a taskmaster. How did you go about discovering that rationale? How did you feel after discovering it?

3. In the absence of motivators, we often greet orders to do a task with a variety of invented demotivators.

When it comes to motivation, few of us experience a neutral middle ground. We feel either motivation to take on the task or demotivation to resist the work at hand. (Such resistance does not mean that we refuse to do the task. We simply do it reluctantly. It is in this context that Thoreau wrote, "Most men live lives of quiet desperation.")

This scenario makes the point. Susan has a small chihuahua, Pepi, whom she sometimes brings to her office for a few hours. Pepi is quiet, friendly, and completely trained. Susan sees no harm in letting him snooze on his blanket under her desk on occasional afternoons. Susan's boss sends her a memo: "Susan, please don't bring your dog into the workplace." Notice that this message is devoid of motivators of any kind. Will Susan tend to think the best of her boss and be positively motivated to comply? Hardly. In the absence of motivators, people tend to make negative assumptions and supply demotivators: "My boss is probably a dog hater. He can't stand any individuality among his employees. He probably thinks I don't work when my dog is with me in the office." On the basis of the demotivators she creates, Susan either resists the order (risking her job) or complies with it unwillingly (risking her productivity).

Suppose none of these demotivators was accurate. The boss sent the memo because the company's insurance policy did not cover animals. If the dog was hurt on company premises, the company could be held liable, with no insurance to pay resulting claims. Because the manager didn't share this motivating information with Susan, she was left in the dark to imagine the worst about her employer and the company.

Lacking other information or insight, we tend to ascribe negative motives and qualities to taskmasters who give us orders we don't like.	**INSIGHT 50**

Your Turn

Tell about a time when you received an order you disliked or resisted. What did you think about the person who gave you the order? Why?

DISCOVERING UNSPOKEN MOTIVATORS

The best taskmasters combine work orders (perhaps phrased as suggestions or requests) with clear motivation. Here are two examples:

- Mr. Robinson wants John to take a class on bookkeeping at the local community college so that John can take over some of the easier tasks now given, at greater cost, to the company accountants. Instead of merely telling John to take the class, Robinson attempts to motivate him: "John, I recognize that you would be taking your own time for this evening class. But once you have bookkeeping skills, I will be able to give you more supervisory responsibilities here at the company. In fact, if you demonstrate your increased value after taking the bookkeeping class, I will consider giving you a significant raise."

  A task that otherwise might make John groan now takes on a different light. He sees the task as a stepping stone to achieving some of his career and financial goals.

- Ms. Rodriguez wants Robert to put more pressure on the six people he supervises to get to work on time. Here's how she combines her order with motivation: "Robert, some of your people continually arrive late to work, sometimes as much as an hour. I want you to communicate to each of your employees that the company won't tolerate this behavior. In fact, I'm setting up a little contest among my supervisors, including you. The supervisor whose group has the best on-time arrival record each quarter will be the guest of honor at a lunch I'll arrange with the boss and executive committee."

  Robert now has a personal interest in seeing that his employees arrive at work on time. By changing the behavior of his people, Robert gets recognition and also gets a chance to rub shoulders with company leaders—certainly an advantage to his career.

However, not all bosses are like Mr. Robinson and Ms. Rodriguez. Many bosses bark out orders with the subtext, "Do it because I told you to." Employees in these situations are often anxious and discontent. Turnover is high as these workers seek more hospitable work environments.

Assume, however, that you're stuck for the time being with a taskmaster—whether in the form of a boss, professor, or organization leader—who neglects to attach motivators to his or her orders. You can refuse to do the task and suffer the consequences. Or, more likely, you can go ahead and do the work with a gripe and grumble.

INSIGHT 51	We often give in to taskmasters and simply do their bidding to avoid conflict.

Your Turn

Describe your feelings after complying with an order or assignment with which you did not agree.

A third alternative, one chosen far too seldom, is to seek out motivators that encourage you to perform the task. These motivators can come from the taskmaster, from you, or from your work group. Let's take each of these motivational sources in turn:

Motivators from the Taskmaster We already have established the scenario of a taskmaster who fails to provide any motivators with an order given to you. It is often the case that taskmasters do have motivators that, if they were known, would provide a boost of energy and morale for those carrying out the order. Why taskmasters fail to provide these motivators is a continuing management riddle. Some taskmasters are simply poor managers and don't understand the power and place of motivation. Other taskmasters consciously withhold motivators as an exercise of power. They practice "management by mystery," keeping their employees in the dark about motives, reasons, and results of work. In this way, these taskmasters reinforce their own power in the organization and disempower their employees.

Although a management-by-mystery taskmaster might not divulge much about motivators to accompany an order, the negligent or untrained taskmaster probably will be somewhat grateful for your inquiries along these lines:

You: "I understand what you want me to do. Does this tie in with the bid we're preparing for the big federal contract?"

Boss: "Exactly. If you can get your piece done on time, we should be in good shape for winning that contract."

Ah, you now have what you need and want: a motivator to perform the job as well as you can. In this case, the motivator is the importance of the job. A major contract depends on your skill. You can take pride in helping achieve the goals of the organization. No doubt your own career path will reflect these contributions.

Your conversation with the boss could have produced many other kinds of motivators:

- Motivation by Reward.

  Boss: "There's a healthy bonus ahead for you if you can get this work done ahead of schedule."

- Motivation by Esteem.

  Boss: "I'm picking you for this task because you're one of my best employees. I know I can count on you."

- Motivation by Expectation.

  Boss: "I've had my eye on the good work you've been doing. Keep it up and there will be gratifying career developments for you in this company."

- Motivation by Fairness.

  Boss: "I know I'm asking you to go beyond your usual job description in doing this job. But give it your best shot during the next couple of weeks and I'll make sure that your workload is lighter than usual during December."

A classic story of seeking the right motivator comes from the history of Apple Computer. Steve Jobs, then leader of the company, was trying his best to coax John Scully to leave his executive position at Pepsico to join Apple. For weeks, Jobs had tried all the typical motivators: financial inducements, perks of all kinds, and a great deal of leadership freedom. None of these motivated Scully to say "yes." Finally, Jobs met with Scully and played his final, and most successful, motivational card. He asked Scully, "Do you really want to make brown sugar water the rest of your life?" This ploy led Scully to think deeply about the social and intellectual importance of what he was doing. He decided to come aboard with Apple Computer and became a legendary corporate leader there.

Taskmasters often can be coaxed to reveal their underlying motives for what otherwise seem to be blunt, unexplained orders.	**INSIGHT 52**

Your Turn

Tell about a favorite manager, supervisor, or other authority figure from your past academic or work life. What did he or she do right in motivating you to achievement?

Motivators from Within Yourself In the previous chapter, we discussed the many kinds of motivators that you carry within. Any of these can be accessed to give you motivational energy to complete the task:

- Motivation by Personality Type.

  You: "This is exactly the kind of job I'm good at. It should be somewhat enjoyable."

- Motivation by Self-Esteem.

  You: "I'm a professional and this task is a small test of what I'm made of. I'll do it right because that's my character."

- Motivation by Mentorship.

  You: "This is the kind of unwelcome task that my dad said I would have to face. And face it I will."

- Motivation by Ambition.

  You: "Doing this task well will be one more step toward a promotion."

INSIGHT 53   Some of our most potent personal motivators are our internalized versions of the influence of outside people.

Your Turn

Consider motivation by ambition. Discuss how this motivation has influenced your attitudes and actions recently.

Motivators from Associates In the same way that individual rowers draw strength from their team-mates on the rowing team, so students or workers at any level can find motivators among their associates.

Here's a quick scenario. Linda is nearing the end of a particularly difficult training program at her company. She dreads the final exam, which she must pass with a score of 80 or higher to do well on her performance evaluation and get a raise. The evening before the test, several members of the training program approach Linda to see if she wants to study with them. Linda at first says "No thanks," thinking that an evening with these people probably will turn into social chat and wasted time. At the same time though, she knows she is exhausted and probably won't get much studying done on her own. She changes her mind and says "yes"—and is pleasantly surprised to find the evening well spent in studying. The commitment and energy of the other members of the program were contagious and provided Linda with motivation to study. She ended up earning a score of 94 on the exam.

Other motivators from associates include the following:

- Motivation by Respect.

    You: "My fellow workers have confidence that I can do this task. If they believe in me, I guess I also can believe in myself."

- Motivation by Loyalty.

    You: "We're all going to look bad if I don't do well on this task. I'm going to do my best for the good of the team."

- Motivation by Friendship.

    You: "I like a lot of my fellow workers and socialize with them often. I think they would feel let down if I blew off this task."

- Motivation by Modeling.

    You: "Others follow my lead. If I do a poor job, they will follow suit."

Whether you tap into motivators from your boss, yourself, or your associates, you have acted in your own best interest to make the task less burdensome, more meaningful, and perhaps more enjoyable.

Our relationships with others, especially with those we like, establish a strong set of personal motivators.	**INSIGHT 54**

	Your Turn

Describe a time when the influence of a group provided the motivation you required to complete a task or activity.

GUARDING YOUR MOTIVATIONAL "BUTTONS"

Authority figures such as bosses and professors sometimes attempt to manipulate those under their charge by repeatedly using certain motivators. The process works like this: Boss A thinks he knows what motivates each of the employees in his group. To his way of thinking, Ralph always will respond to promises of a future reward of some kind; Jill will respond to heaps of praise; Reginald will respond to being told that he is special among the group, and so forth for the rest of the employees.

By becoming too dependent on any one motivator—and letting others observe our dependence—we set ourselves up for manipulation. We guard against such abuse by becoming aware of *many* of the motivators that are powerful for us. With this complex view of our personal motivators in mind, we easily will spot someone who attempts to use one motivator over and over as a way of controlling our behavior.

INSIGHT 55	When others know our primary motivators, they might misuse them as a way of controlling us.

Your Turn

People who know you well also know what motivates you. Has anyone ever used such knowledge in a way you did not like? If so, tell about the experience and what you learned. If not, tell how you prevent others from "pushing your buttons."

Summing Up

From our earliest years, a succession of taskmasters tells us what to do and how to feel. Often, we internalize the voices of these taskmasters so that eventually we are unsure whether their agendas or our own are being acted upon. Learning to find the rationale behind a taskmaster's orders takes us beyond blind obedience to a position of understanding and choice. In addition to taskmasters, friends and associates influence our set of personal motivators.

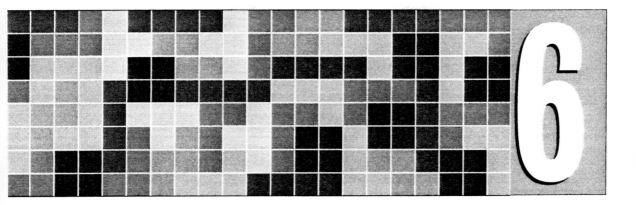

Motivation by Reward

GOALS

- Grasp the broad range of rewards that influence our personal motivation.
- Evaluate the relative worth of these rewards to our best interests.
- Transform external reward systems into internal rewards that we can use for self-motivation.

"Wanted—Large Reward Offered." That formula has worked for apprehending criminals for hundreds of years. More recently, it has been used to motivate behavior as various as executive head-hunting (in which the employment agent receives a fee for finding the right job candidate), technological breakthroughs (in which scientific achievements are rewarded by company bonuses, the Nobel prize, and so forth), and recovery of missing property or pets.

With a bit of tweaking, this classic formula can be useful to your efforts in locating personal motivators that encourage achievement.

WHAT DO YOU WANT?

The first part of the formula—"Wanted"—gives a detailed description of the thing or act for which the reward is offered. If that description is vague, the chances of attaining it are reduced. As a simple example, a vague description of a lost pet ("a dog with a short tail") makes the process of finding the sought-after pet difficult if not impossible. In the same way, an unfocused description of what you seek makes the attainment of that goal unlikely.

- "I want a better job." (vague); "I want a job that makes use of my financial skills and pays at least 20 percent better than my present job." (specific)
- "I want more education." (vague); "I want to finish my undergraduate degree and complete the necessary examinations for my stock broker's license." (specific)
- "I want to work more with people." (vague); "I want a work environment where I'm a member of a work team and where I have direct contact with customers." (specific)

Your ability to be specific about what you want puts you in a good position to define rewards that will motivate you to reach that goal.

INSIGHT 56   Stating what one wants in specific terms increases the likelihood of getting it.

Your Turn

Describe one thing or experience you want. Be as specific as possible. What personal motivators are most likely to help you reach your goal?

HOW WILL YOU REWARD YOURSELF?

The idea of rewarding yourself might seem odd at first. We probably are more used to looking to others for our rewards: payment from our bosses, grades from our professors, approval from our friends, and so forth. As effective as these rewards might be in motivating our behavior, this book focuses on a different class of rewards: those that you can use to motivate *yourself* to achievement.

The advantage, of course, of developing and using a system of personal rewards is that you aren't forever waiting on others to recognize what you are doing well. That waiting process can kill motivation and our enthusiasm for activities at work or in our social lives. Some bosses are notorious for delaying praise for employee performance or neglecting it altogether. Some people wait well into adulthood in expectation that a parent finally will give a reward in the form of approval, encouragement, or expressions of love.

There's little waiting with a well-practiced system of personal rewards. The process of giving oneself rewards is straightforward:

- Begin by determining which behaviors require the motivating support of a reward. Define those behaviors (including changes in behavior) specifically.
- Find a reward that is suitable in importance and scale to the goal you have set for yourself. (The reward of a new car, for example, isn't appropriately matched to the achievement of choosing nonfat milk instead of cream for your coffee.)
- Follow through as conscientiously in rewarding yourself as you would in rewarding others for reaching an agreed-upon goal.

| The nature of a personal reward must be in keeping with the behavior being rewarded. | **INSIGHT 57** |

| **Your Turn** |
| Recall the last time you rewarded yourself for some achievement or accomplishment. What did you do to earn the reward? How did you select the reward? How did you feel after rewarding yourself? |

A scenario might make the process of self-reward more approachable.

Juan desperately wants to lose 20 pounds in order to feel better about himself and be more confident in his social contacts. As he thinks about his past life, he has celebrated past achievements (that is, rewarded himself) primarily by eating rich food in large quantities. For example, when he got his last promotion, his friends took him out to a lavish dinner. His birthdays had been celebrated for as long as he could remember with cake and ice cream. Those rewards, however motivating they were in the past, obviously were not well suited to Juan's diet plans.

He thought about his options. On one hand, he could pay an outside weight-loss organization to provide rewards for him. For a fee, he could count on this company to provide a coach who would praise him for each ounce he shed and other dieters to clap for him as he stood on the scale. Alternately, Juan could hope that his friends would notice his gradual loss of weight and, in effect, reward him by telling him how fit and slim he was looking.

Neither of these options appealed to Juan. He didn't want to pay someone for what he was losing (pounds), and he didn't trust his friends to speak up on a regular basis with the kind of encouragement he needed to stick to his diet. Juan therefore reviewed his own list of personal motivators (other than eating). At the top of his list, he realized, was travel. In his view, he had traveled too little in his life and earnestly wanted to see more of the world. Juan's deal with himself took shape as follows: "If I lose 20 pounds and keep it off for 60 days, I will take a Caribbean vacation—and commit to an exercise program and active participation in water sports while I'm there."

To keep himself on track, Juan taped postcards of Caribbean beaches and sunsets to his refrigerator. He achieved his weight reduction goal on schedule and enjoyed the personal reward of his vacation immensely.

INSIGHT 58	A perpetually available, specifically described vision of the goal is a key component in achieving it.

Your Turn	
When you have sought a particular goal, what have you done to keep it fresh in your mind and at the top of your priorities?	

CONVERTING OUTSIDE REWARDS TO INNER REWARDS

As Juan's experience suggests, personal rewards can be effective motivators for at least three reasons:

1. Personal rewards are well chosen. We know (or should know) better than anyone else what motivates us. The reward we settle on has the best chance of motivating the achievement we seek.

2. Personal rewards are predictable. Control over when, where, and how our reward is given lies entirely in our own power.

3. The personal reward system is repeatable. Once we discover that we can motivate ourselves through rewards for achievement (in Jung's phrase, "water the tree"), we can use this approach over and over to reach personal and professional goals.

Rewards from the outside often come with strings attached. Rewards presented to oneself can be tailored to avoid such unnecessary complications and obligations.

INSIGHT 59

Your Turn

Think of some goal or achievement for which you are now working. What rewards have you considered to celebrate your eventual accomplishment? Which of these rewards is most motivating to you? Why?

Because the process of self-reward is new for many people, it might be helpful to spell out some of the most common rewards used for personal motivation. Notice that each of the following rewards is nothing more than a personalized version of a reward more familiarly bestowed on us by outsiders:

Approval. We are motivated to work for this reward from our earliest childhood days. Some of our behaviors pleased Mom and Dad and earned signs of their approval (in the form of smiles, hugs, kind words, treats, and so on). Other behaviors provoked the withholding of approval or the substitution of signs of disapproval (too traumatic to recount). At some point in our preadolescent development, we began to approve of certain aspects of ourselves. We might have liked the way we looked or played sports or sang songs. In subtle and not-so-subtle ways, we took pride in these aspects of our lives and gave ourselves approval for them. (Note that those who never achieved this plateau of self-approval were doomed to face the suffering of complete dependency on others for approval. Friends, spouses, and even parents can wilt under the unending burden of trying to make someone else feel OK.)

We can individually harness the power of approval by completing thoughts such as the following:

"It makes me feel good when I . . . "
"I am proud of myself when I . . . "
"I'm happiest when I . . . "

The responses to these prompts are usually activities of some kind: "It makes me feel good when I share my good fortune with others." "I am proud of myself when I exercise regularly." "I'm happiest when I achieve a goal I've worked hard for."

Once those activities are on the table, it's crucially important to ask the question, "Why do I experience self-approval during and after these activities?"

In the case of sharing good fortune, the answer might be as follows: "I approve of myself because I'm living up to my personal values." In the case of maintaining an exercise regimen, the answer might be "I approve of myself because I'm doing what I can to be healthy and attractive." In the case of achieving goals, the answer might be "I approve of myself because I'm able to succeed in meeting personal challenges."

INSIGHT 60	Learning to approve of oneself rather than relying exclusively on others for approval is a sign of growing maturity.

Your Turn	
In what ways do you tell yourself that you approve of what you do and how you feel?	

Money. The most common reward symbol in industrialized societies is cash. It's important to recognize the symbolic value of this reward: paper or bits of circular metal convey no reward in and of themselves. They must be translated (or be able to be translated) into desired rewards—food, travel, homes, clothing, cars, college tuition, charitable donations—before they have any motivational power at all. At times of disastrous inflation, money can lose much of its value as a reward. People probably have quit stooping for stray pennies—and now nickels and dimes—for just this reason. The effort of acquiring the coins surpasses the value or enjoyment of what they can buy.

In business, money is used most frequently as the carrot dangling before the eager noses of workers. To keep these employees interested in the reward—and, ideally, increasingly interested—companies gradually change the size of the carrot. If that change is too gradual, employee motivation falls off. A small raise every 3 or 4 years hardly encourages best effort. On the other hand, if the carrot grows too large too quickly, the company might be unable to keep pace with the employees' expectations. A 50 percent raise every month would thrill the employees but quickly bankrupt the company.

A middle ground usually is found in which money rewards are somewhat less than the employee would wish (but not discouragingly so) and somewhat more than the company would like to pay. At times, raises are used by companies as status motivators. Fast-food companies frequently offer small raises—25 cents or less per hour—within a month or two of the employee's hiring date. The amount itself is rather insignificant in its translation into buying power, but the status (in the eyes of parents, friends, and coworkers) of getting one raise, then another, then another in a relatively short time span can be highly motivating, especially for teens new to the world of work.

In determining how to turn the power of money rewards to personal use, we can discard the unwieldy notion of literally paying ourselves for progress toward a personal goal. Few people will bother to take money out of one envelope or account and place it in the "personal reward" piggy bank.

However, we can make use of money as a personal motivator in this way:

1. Do a monthly budget (a rough cut will do).

2. Put a star beside any category on the budget that you consider pleasure spending. These selections will vary according to individual but might include nonessential clothes shopping, restaurant and entertainment expenses, vacation travel, hobby expenses, and so forth.

3. Strike a deal with yourself as follows: "I will cut back on pleasure spending in category X by (specify a dollar amount or percentage) until I have achieved my goal of (specify your desired achievement)."

Here's a scenario of the process:
Victor wants to motivate himself to achieve a 3.5 grade point average by the end of the semester. He notes on his monthly budget that he spends about $100 each month on movies and movie rentals. This category definitely qualifies as pleasure spending for Victor—he loves movies and would willingly spend much more per month on them if he had the money. Victor commits to cutting back his movie expenses to $50 per month until he achieves his goal of a 3.5 grade point average. Victor reasons that once he reaches his goal, the return to $100 for movies will seem like a luxury and a fitting reward for his effort. Victor also realizes that cutting back on movies will give him more time to study.

This approach of denial and restoration of spending is more practical for most people than rewarding ourselves simply by increased pleasure spending. Imagine in Victor's case if he had structured his motivating reward as $200 per month for movies—extra money he didn't have, and hence a reward that, however attractive, was foolish and unworkable.

Money is a symbol for our ability to access pleasure and security for ourselves and others.	**INSIGHT 61**

Your Turn
Tell about a time when you used some form of monetary reward to motivate yourself.

Status. This motivator is sufficiently strong to keep entry-level employees in corporate jobs with their noses to the grindstone in an effort to pay their dues and climb the first rungs of the corporate ladder toward more elevated status. Gangs use this same motivator to demand outrageous acts from those seeking to join: rob a convenience store (or worse) to gain the status of membership. In some organizations including banks, changes in status often are used instead of monetary rewards to motivate loyalty and performance. Some banks have a plethora of assistant vice presidents, vice presidents, senior vice presidents, and executive vice presidents for whom status of title is apparently more motivating than salary levels.

Turning the power of status to personal use might appear problematic at first. Isn't status by definition a reward given by outsiders, whether gang leaders or bank directors? Not necessarily. Consider the personalized use of status in this scenario.

Burton worked his way through college by taking virtually any job he could find. He shoveled snow, babysat, flipped burgers, performed handyman chores, raked leaves, sorted library books, and cleaned offices. All the while he was pursuing a degree in accounting. Burton made one promise to himself in his college years: On the day of his graduation, he would consider himself an accountant and, come what may, would only take jobs in line with his goals for that profession.

Status, in this case, was a strong motivator for Burton—something to live and work for. At the same time, status was largely self-bestowed. Although the college gave him a degree in accounting, only Burton could make the motivating decision in terms of his self-image to declare himself an accountant. The same internal commitment to status can be said of aspiring actors—against all odds, they define themselves as members of that profession, even while having to drive cabs or wait tables to make ends meet.

| INSIGHT 62 | Status is an inner recognition of who we are, not a gift that is bestowed on us from external sources. |

| Your Turn | |

How would you describe your status at present? How do you want it to change in the future?

THE TIMING OF REWARDS

To be truly motivational, rewards cannot be put off forever. "What happens to a dream deferred?" asks Langston Hughes, only to decide later in the familiar poem that the postponed dream explodes.

Many motivators used by teachers during our school years had little lasting effect because of a timing problem. While studying geometry, we might have been assured by the teacher that "you will need this someday." For a portion of the class, that "someday" did eventually come—but many years after the laborious work of memorizing theorems and corollaries. As a general rule, the reward itself or some portion of the reward should follow quickly upon the completion of work leading to that reward. Common sense tells us that we wouldn't work long for a boss who promised to pay us a year or more after we had completed our labor.

The timing of rewards is crucial to their motivational influence.	**INSIGHT 63**

Your Turn
Describe a time when the timing of a reward you received or gave to yourself interfered with its motivational influence. What timing would have been better? Why?

Therefore, in deciding how to reward yourself as a means of self-motivation, also consider *when* to reward yourself. Here are two scenarios, the first illustrating the motivational danger of too much instant gratification and the second indicating the motivational danger of rewards delayed too long.

A tale of instant gratification. To move ahead in his job, Todd had to master the training manual for a new machine, the X7C. The manual, to his dismay, was more than 300 pages long—and written in a dense, encyclopedic style. Todd found himself nodding off after reading even a few pages. "I need motivation," Todd decided. His scheme was as follows: "I will pay myself a dollar for every five pages I read. By the time I'm done with the manual, I'll have enough to buy several of the CDs I've wanted." The motivation system worked at first. Todd read the first five pages and promptly paid himself a dollar. Reading the second five pages also seemed somewhat easier because of the dollar strategy. But by page 30 or so, Todd had tired completely of his reward system. "I sit here thinking about getting through five pages and daydreaming about CDs instead of focusing on the manual," he admitted to himself. The reward he had settled on was too trivial and came too often to sustain his effort through the long manual.

Sustained instant gratification detracts from the power of long-term motivators.	**INSIGHT 64**

Your Turn

In what aspects of American life do you observe the influence of instant gratification as a motivator? In your opinion, what is the result or outcome of such instant gratification?

A tale of delayed gratification. Linda, Todd's work associate, faced the daunting task of reading the same training manual with which Todd was struggling. "To motivate myself," Linda thought to herself, "I will take a trip sometime to Hawaii—maybe next year. I've always wanted to go there." Within a few dozen pages of reading, however, Linda found that the abstract, delayed nature of her self-motivator was providing hardly any sense of urgency or energy to finish the manual. "Next year is a long way off," she complained to herself. "Hawaii is just a distant dream."

INSIGHT 65

Delayed gratification can delay or derail motivation.

Your Turn

Describe a time when you promised yourself a reward that later proved to be out of reach. What effect did that fact have on your motivation?

Summing Up

Rewards, and the pleasure they bring with them, are central to the process of motivation. Although many rewards are given from external sources, it is wise to learn how to reward oneself for achievements. These self-given bonuses can include approval, money, and status rewards. When and how rewards are given is crucial to the success of those rewards.

Motivation by What You Expect

GOALS

- Understand how we use imagined future achievement or contentment as a spur to present action.

- Grasp the relationship between goal-directed and goal-fulfillment activities.

- Recognize that motivation through expectation can be distorted in a pursuit of illusions.

This chapter explores the profound influence our expectations for the future have on us. In one way or another, we all labor intensely in the belief (mixed with hope) that our efforts will yield a better tomorrow, however that future is defined.

Try this brief experiment. List five activities in which you've been involved in the last few days. For each activity, think of its "expectation component"—that is, what you expect or hope that activity will lead to in the short- or long-term future. We asked one college senior in business school, Samantha, to conduct this experiment. Here is her list of five activities:

1. Research company XYZ in preparation for a job interview there.

2. Contact the trainer at the gym to discuss a personal fitness program.

3. Transfer my high-interest credit card balance to a new card with a lower interest rate.

4. See if my boyfriend is available for a date this weekend.

5. Pick out and mail a birthday gift to my younger sister.

Under examination, each of these items had a substantial expectation component, stated here in Samantha's perspective:

1. "If I learn a lot about the company, I will have a better chance of getting hired."

2. "Part of the reason I feel tired is my lack of exercise. If I get onto a regular exercise program, I'll feel better about myself and have more energy."

3. "By transferring my balance to a new card, I'll save at least $30 in interest charges each month."

4. "There's a movie I've been dying to see."

5. "I can picture her face when she opens this gift!"

Samantha is highly motivated—and self-motivated—to perform each of these activities because she is convinced that the activities will yield benefits in the future. One way to demonstrate the power of this expectancy component as a motivator for Samantha is to take it away. Would she research the company if she believed the effort would have no influence on her chances for a job? Would she bother to contact the trainer at the gym if she believed that exercise would have no effect on how she felt and looked? Would she transfer her credit card balance to a new card if she gained no benefit by doing so? In all cases, of course not. Samantha's *imagined future* for each of these activities provides the personal fuel and enthusiasm she needs to carry them through.

INSIGHT 66	By expecting good things in our future, we motivate ourselves to work toward those imagined rewards.

Name one or two of your most cherished expectations for the future. In what ways are those expectations motivating you now? Be as specific as possible.

GOAL-DIRECTED ACTIVITIES LEADING TO GOAL-FULFILLMENT ACTIVITIES

The expectancy component in self-motivation can be dissected into two equally important halves as shown in Figure 7.1.

The first half in this diagram, Goal-Directed Activities, includes all those things we do (including our thinking, planning, and hoping) in an effort to reach our goal or reward. The second half of the diagram, Goal-Fulfillment Activities, includes all the pleasure or celebration activities that come as the result of our successful Goal-Directed Activities.

As we mature, we move from smaller to larger Goal-Directed Activities; that is, we are willing to do more and more *in expectation of* our eventual reward. You recall, perhaps, from an introductory psychology or biology class the experiment with the pecking chicken and a bell. In this classic conditioning demonstration, a chicken accidentally bumps into a small bell near its feeding tray. As the bell rings, a grain of corn drops into the tray and the chicken eats it. After several unsuccessful attempts to get more corn, the chicken bumps the bell again and, sure enough, a grain of corn appears and is promptly eaten. Now the chicken has a clue (however dim) about how to get corn. The chicken pecks the bell and a grain of corn appears. This process is repeated over and over, to the chicken's delight.

Then things change. The chicken rings the bell and no grain appears. The chicken, probably as confused as a chicken can be, pecks again and—happily—a grain of corn appears. However, as the experiment continues, the

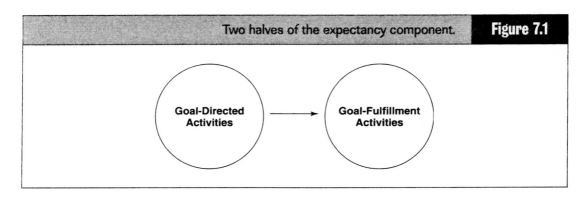

Two halves of the expectancy component.   **Figure 7.1**

Goal-Directed Activities → Goal-Fulfillment Activities

grain of corn comes less and less predictably in relation to the ringing of the bell. Here's the key question that interested researchers in operant conditioning and applies no less to our discussion of self-motivation: How many times will the chicken ring the bell in expectation of a reward before giving up in discouragement? The answer, you might recall, was surprising: The chicken (and a variety of other animals) would repeat an activity hundreds of times if it at some point led to the desired reward (i.e., eating the grain of corn, or, in our previous terms, the Goal-Fulfillment Activities).

A somewhat comical human version of this same experiment involves people who incessantly check the change slot of pay telephones in hopes of finding a stray nickel, dime, or quarter. How many telephones will they check in the course of a week for their reward of probably less than a dollar in change? Often a person who's hooked on checking pay phones will scoop a finger through dozens of empty coin slots before finding one that has a coin in it. That one though (the Goal-Fulfillment Activity or "grain of corn") is apparently enough to sustain the habit and motivate the checking of dozens of other phones.

INSIGHT 67	We learn to devote more energy to goal-directed activities as long as we believe we can achieve desired goal-fulfillment activities.

Your Turn	
Think of some situation in your present life in which you are performing many goal-directed activities. What are the goal-fulfillment activities that will accompany these goal-directed activities? When will the goal-fulfillment activities begin? How do you feel about the relationship between these two kinds of activities?	

What's going on to motivate all this endeavor for such infrequent and meager reward? Motivation researcher Victor Vroom has helped us understand the inner workings of expectancy motivation with his three-part formula shown in Figure 7.2.

OLIVER IN TROUBLE

We can capture the wisdom of this formula in a scenario from work life. First, let's investigate a situation in which a worker is demotivated precisely because he fails each of Vroom's three linked tests for motivation. Then we

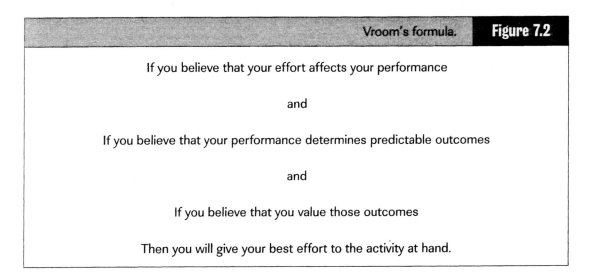

Vroom's formula. **Figure 7.2**

If you believe that your effort affects your performance

and

If you believe that your performance determines predictable outcomes

and

If you believe that you value those outcomes

Then you will give your best effort to the activity at hand.

will play back the scenario to show how compliance with Vroom's three standards produces almost-unlimited motivation.

Here's the circumstance. Oliver, a new employee at XYZ Corporation, is deeply discouraged. "I'm supposed to be writing computer code," he says, "but I've never had training in the kind of code they use at this company. No matter how hard I try—and I'm trying very hard—I just can't get it right." Notice here that Oliver is failing Vroom's first motivation test: He does not believe that his effort affects his performance. As many workers complain, "I'm working as hard as I can but getting nowhere."

Oliver eventually catches on to writing appropriate computer code but now runs into a second problem at the company: "There's no logic to who gets paid what around here," Oliver complains. "Some of the people I work with do virtually nothing all day, but they get paid the same as or more than I do. One of them just got promoted!" Here Oliver is failing Vroom's second standard for motivation: Oliver doesn't believe that his performance will lead to predictable outcomes. Whether he works well or works poorly seems unimportant to his supervisor and the company.

Finally, Oliver hits the wall at the end of the discouragement road. He gets his paycheck, sneers at the amount on the check, and says, "How can I afford to live on this measly pay? Does the company know how much rent, food, and transportation cost in this city? I can barely afford to rent a bedroom on what I'm getting paid—and I'm not about to live in a bedroom in someone else's house!"

Here Oliver fails the last of Vroom's standards for motivation. He does not value the outcome of his performance. Oliver's professional life from this point on is probably dreary to recount. He might hang on at the company for a matter of weeks or months, but he is deeply unhappy with his situation and has no reason to do a good job, or even try, on projects assigned to him.

INSIGHT 68	Personal motivation has key components that must each be present for motivation to be effective.

Your Turn	

Put yourself in Oliver's situation. What would you do first to reverse the downward spiral of his motivation?

SAVING OLIVER—OR, WATCHING OLIVER SAVE HIMSELF

To restore his motivation, Oliver has only to remodel his Goal-Directed and Goal-Fulfillment Activities (a task easier said than done). In the following scenario, he succeeds at each of Vroom's three standards for motivation; this difference produces success.

First, Oliver must believe that his effort affects his performance. "I'm learning a new form of computer code for use in this company," Oliver tells himself, "and when I master it, I'll be able to do my job as a programmer at a high level of skill." As predicted, within a couple of weeks, Oliver has learned the new code and is performing well for the company.

Next, Oliver must believe that his performance determines predictable outcomes. "If I continue to do my job this well," Oliver tells himself, "I'll not only be kept on as an employee but will put myself in line for bonuses and promotions. That's the way it works at this company. Performance is always rewarded." Again, Oliver's progress is swift. Within a year, he is lead programmer for his group and has added 30 percent to his starting salary.

Finally, Oliver must value the outcome of his performance. "With my new raise, I will be able to save enough in the next year to make a down payment on my own condo or maybe a small house. That's always been my dream—to have my own home. Who knows? Maybe marriage and kids are next."

INSIGHT 69	The relationship among effort, performance, predictable outcomes, and valuation of those outcomes determines the potency of personal motivation.

Describe an experience in which your motivation was less than you wanted it to be. Using Vroom's formula, diagnose what went wrong with your motivation and what could have been done to make it stronger.

USING VROOM'S FORMULA FOR PERSONAL ASSESSMENT

If your motivation level for a particular activity is running on empty, you often can discover not only what's wrong but also how to make it right again by reviewing Vroom's three standards. For example, suppose you are struggling through a particular college class. It's not difficult work, but you're having a terrible time keeping up with the reading and frequent assignments. You recognize that you have a motivational problem with the class.

Here's the kind of self-assessment you can do, based on Vroom's three steps:

1. "Let's see, do I think that my effort affects my performance in this class? Yeah, I guess so. I know that I can ace the class if I put in the work."

2. "Do I think that my performance will lead to predictable outcomes? Definitely. The professor is fair and assigns grades according to what you have earned."

3. "So, my motivation problem must lie in the last step: Do I really value the outcome of a good grade in the class? That's exactly the problem. The class isn't in my major and I'm taking it just so I can graduate."

Once the problem is located (here, in step 3), the solution can be found, as well: "I have to value the outcome of my performance. Even if I don't like the content of the class, I can value the effect of a good grade on my overall grade point average. In fact, if I get an A in this class, I will have the kind of grade point average that might get me a fellowship for graduate school. Now I have a reason to do well in the class!"

This self-assessment along the lines of Vroom's three standards probably is unusually clear cut. Untangling real-world discouragements can take much more soul-searching. However, the underlying point remains valid: Motivation has defined parts, all linked to produce eventual encouragement or discouragement. Reviewing those parts as they apply to our individual circumstances gives us an excellent chance of discovering the roots of and remedies for our occasional lack of motivation.

| **INSIGHT 70** | We can diagnose failures of motivation by discovering components that are flawed. |

| **Your Turn** | |

Vroom asserts that we must believe our performance leads to predictable outcomes in order for motivation to be maximized. Do you agree? Give an example from your own school or work life to support your point.

RISING TO THE CHALLENGE

Motivation researchers have discovered another fascinating phenomenon about the motivators that energize human activity. Consider these research questions:

- If you knew with certainty that you would succeed at an activity no matter what your level of effort or focus was, how strong would your motivation be to undertake and continue the activity?
- If you knew with certainty that you would fail at an activity no matter what your level of effort or focus was, how strong would your motivation be to undertake and continue that activity?

Your answer is probably the same for both questions: Motivation would be weak indeed in both cases. As expressed in the "50 percent curve," shown in Figure 7.3, made famous by researchers David C. McClelland and John W. Atkinson, motivation rises with the degree of challenge and falls off only when it appears that the challenge is increasingly overwhelming:

Put in plain language, we don't bother trying when success in an activity is a sure thing; nor do we try when we don't have a chance. We reach our maximum level of motivation when our likelihood of success or failure is peaking.

This pattern of motivation is apparent to anyone who has watched a few baseball games. When the score is 10 to 0, the losing team goes through the motions of the game but doesn't act as if it really has a chance of winning and doesn't put forth maximum effort. Similarly, when the score is 20 to 0, the winners relax and often put in the B team to play the remainder of the game. Only when the score is, perhaps, 2 to 2 in the final innings of the game do we see each player exerting maximum skill and effort to produce a winning result.

As another example, consider throwing cards into a hat. If you get each card you throw into the hat every time, you soon lose interest in the game. (Or, you create interest only by showing your skill to those who don't believe you can get the cards in the hat every time.) If you never get a card in

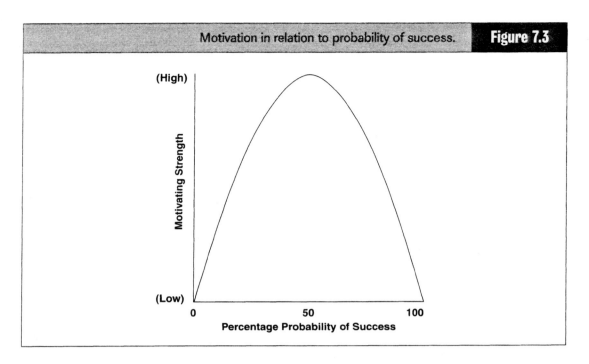

Motivation in relation to probability of success.   **Figure 7.3**

the hat deck after deck, the game also loses its appeal. (You can't attract a crowd to this display of nonskill, unless you find a crowd made up of people who believe you will get each card in the hat and are amazed at your display of stunning incompetence.)

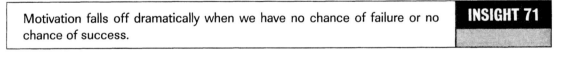

Motivation falls off dramatically when we have no chance of failure or no chance of success.   **INSIGHT 71**

Your Turn

Describe one of your experiences in which you knew from the beginning that you would succeed. How would you characterize your motivation for this experience?

USING THE CHALLENGE PHENOMENON IN SELF-MOTIVATION

One implication of the challenge phenomenon is to be realistic with yourself when you face an impossible task. Instead of questioning what's wrong with yourself, it's sane and practical to face the facts: "My motivation is obviously low because I don't believe I have any chance of success. There's little to be gained in blaming myself for low motivation. My energy will be better spent trying to change the situation itself in some way so that I do have a chance at success."

The corollary of the no-chance scenario is the sure-thing problem: "I'm completely bored with what I'm doing because it is so easy. I could do this job in my sleep. Is this all there is?" This recognition of low motivation stems from the other end of the 50 percent curve. When tasks become rote and uninteresting, we have a strong signal to assess our motivation to continue those tasks. Even if we thought ease and constant success at tasks would be our dream job, we might find ourselves surprised at the degree to which we need a bit of challenge to keep life and work interesting.

Some companies that use this knowledge about motivation rotate key managers to new positions every few years. Thrown into new situations, these managers find their zest for professional life renewed by the increased degree of challenge and opportunity.

INSIGHT 72	Challenges, as long as they are not impossible, invite strong motivation.

Your Turn	

Describe an experience in which you were challenged to exert your best effort. Did you believe you had a reasonable chance of succeeding? How would you describe your motivation level in meeting this challenge? What was the specific type or source of your motivation?

DREAMING OUR LIVES AWAY

Is there such as thing as too much reliance on expectancy motivation? Answer that question for yourself by considering the following scenario.

Cindy took at job as a secretarial assistant below her ability level and pay expectations at PQR Company. She did so, she explained, to get a foot inside the door of the company. She was sure that her future there would be bright if she could just have a chance to show what she could do. In the course of her first year, Cindy was undoubtedly the best secretarial assistant the company had ever had. She won an award at year's end, in fact, as Secretarial Assistant of the Year. Cindy's motivation came not from her day-to-day activities—mostly filing and word processing—but from her fervent belief that her talents would be discovered at some point in the near future. She waited for an e-mail or memo from the boss—the message she had envisioned so often: "Cindy, you are management material." However, when that message didn't arrive after her second year at the company, and still serving as a secretarial assistant, she began to have nagging doubts. Was she doing something wrong? Did she have enemies in the company? Her doubts plagued her to such an extent that she sat down with her supervisor for a heart-to-heart conversation. "No, Cindy," the supervisor reassured her, "your work has been fantastic, as usual. And I don't know of anyone in the company who doesn't think very highly of you."

"Then why," Cindy blurted, "hasn't someone asked me to apply for an upper-level job? It's obvious that I'm smart enough." Her supervisor took a deep breath and replied, "Cindy, in this company assistant secretaries don't become managers. That may not be fair, but it's the way things have always been here and will probably remain. It's the same thing in college, isn't it? Secretaries don't become professors, no matter how many classes they take. And no matter what you see in the movies, people who work in the mailroom don't gradually rise to top management positions."

Cindy began to blame the company for its rigid, unfair attitudes. However, at the same time she had to accept some of the responsibility for her problem. She had fueled her enthusiasm for work tasks by her dream of what would occur in the future—expectations, it turns out, that were entirely unrealistic.

When we motivate ourselves by expectation, we run the risk of deceiving ourselves about unrealistic future rewards.	**INSIGHT 73**

Your Turn
Tell about a person who, in your opinion, had or has unrealistic expectations for the future. What do you foresee will be the outcome of these expectations? What will be the impact on the person?

Cindy's story aside, the message for all of us who are motivated in part by our expectations for tomorrow (or the day after) is to examine those expectations carefully and realistically. Three questions will help guide that examination:

- *In specific terms, what do I think the future result will be of my present efforts?* (It's easy to be vague—"a better job," "more time for myself"—but the goal here is to describe the desired future in as much detail as possible. Exactly what are you working toward?)

- *What is my acceptable time line for future rewards?* Are you willing to wait hours, days, weeks, months, or years for the future you're working toward? Will you accept partial rewards along the way? Of what sort? How will you know when the desired future isn't arriving as you had hoped?

- *What evidence do I have that my expectation is possible?* Cindy, in our earlier story, should have investigated the company to see if any secretaries had ever moved beyond their general job category and, if so, how and when. If we find ourselves believing that we are the only humans (out of almost 6 billion at present) to attain a particular future, we're in danger of kidding ourselves. (State lotteries are based on just such human foibles. Unfortunately, those least able to assess their chances accurately in such games of bad odds are those who spend the greatest percentage of their income on them.)

If we can answer these three questions to our satisfaction, there's every reason to use expectation (as contained in our ambitions, daydreams, and fantasies) to motivate our individual enthusiasm and performance. In Browning's stirring words, "A man's reach must exceed his grasp/Or what's a heaven for?"

INSIGHT 74	Evaluation of our expectations based on specificity, timing, and precedent or evidence protects us against pursuing illusory rewards.

Your Turn

Call to mind one of your future expectations. Describe your own process for determining whether this expectation is realistic and achievable.

Summing Up

Our optimism for possible rewards in the future provides a powerful set of motivators for present action. The components of motivation based on expectation involve effort, performance, predictable outcomes, and valued rewards. Properly linked, these components ensure strong motivation. To guard against self-deception, our expectations for the future should be evaluated on the basis of their specificity, timing, and precedents or evidence.

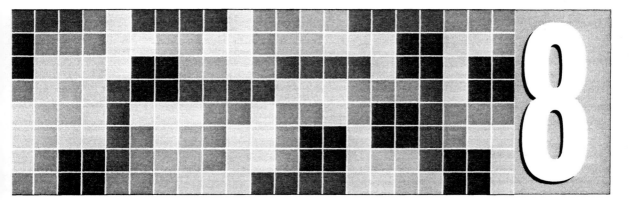

Motivation by What's Fair

GOALS

- Grasp the power of fairness to motivate.
- Understand ways in which we attempt to influence the "fairness equation."
- Consider strategies to keep our desire for fairness from preventing the pursuit of our best interests.

Many expressions in English refer to fairness:

- "What's good for the goose is good for the gander."
- "What goes around comes around."
- "Do unto others as you would have others do unto you."

All these sayings describe a world in which justice operates—or should operate. This chapter is about that sense of justice and how it can be harnessed by each of us as a powerful motivator. On the flip side, we also will see that when we believe justice is absent, we can become demotivated indeed.

WHEN THE SCALES OF JUSTICE GO AWRY

No reader of this book can fail to remember at least one example of unfairness at school or work. In retrospect, these are often among the most memorable and perhaps painful incidents. A teacher at some point might have accused us unjustly of some infraction against academic rules and punished us by a reduced grade or other sanction. "It's unfair!" we howled at the time to ourselves, our friends, and whoever else would listen. An employer might have overlooked our hard work and rewarded someone else in the organization—someone we knew contributed far less than we did to the company. "It's unfair!" we again complained.

On some of these occasions, our anger might have emboldened us to risky activity: bluntly telling the teacher what we thought of him or her; accusing a boss of favoritism or other bias; and perhaps quitting our project, team, or job in a huff. One reason that unfairness cuts so deeply and arouses such passion is that it undercuts most of our other motivators. For example, our motivation to step ahead in our career through hard work is cut to shreds if the "system" doesn't value hard work. Our efforts to learn new job responsibilities on our own time are similarly made meaningless if the boss gives greater rewards to those who resist new ideas and scoff at new skills. We feel professionally imperiled at such moments. Our way of getting ahead or at least keeping even has been sabotaged. We react with a mixture of outrage, disappointment, and anger.

INSIGHT 75	Our feelings about unfairness directly influence the type and level of our motivation.

Your Turn	
Describe a time when a lack of fairness caused a reduction in your motivation. What was the outcome of the situation?	

Sometimes our reaction causes the scales of justice to wobble back into balance. In other words, bosses, professors, and others occasionally see the error of their ways and act to correct the injustice. However, more often our anger changes nothing in the academic or work world. We are left to nurse our wounds and bore our friends with stories of what others did wrong. This cycle of expectation, disappointment, then simmering anger can be repeated over the course of a career to the point that we become cynical about the intentions of all authority figures and the organizations they represent. "Take care of Number One" is a familiar saying among experienced corporate workers—"number one" being the individual.

> Repeated encounters with unfair environments can breed cynicism and permanently cripple motivation.   **INSIGHT 76**

> **Your Turn**
>
> Describe a time when you acted to repair an unfair situation. What did you try to do? Were you successful? Why or why not?

BALANCING THE SCALES OF JUSTICE

J. Stacy Adams, a famed motivation and management researcher, proposed a helpful formula, shown in Figure 8.1, for understanding the balance and fairness we seek at school and in the workplace. We usually apply this formula on an apples-for-apples basis; that is, making our comparison within one organization or work group. If we start making comparisons between companies or different professions, the scales begin to seem meaningless. For example, a janitor in one company usually does not try to work out the fairness equation by comparing the janitorial job with that of a physician working for a health maintenance organization.

Translated into a brief scenario, Adams's fairness or equity equation works out as follows.

Jane holds a bachelor of arts in marketing and works a 40-hour week in the product promotion department of a major corporation. She earns $65,000 per year and gets a 2-week paid vacation annually. Her boss,

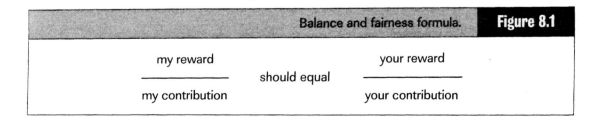

Balance and fairness formula.   **Figure 8.1**

$$\frac{\text{my reward}}{\text{my contribution}} \quad \text{should equal} \quad \frac{\text{your reward}}{\text{your contribution}}$$

Wendy, has her master's in business administration and also works at least a 40-hour week as department head. Jane knows that Wendy gets a 3-week paid vacation each year and earns $95,000 annually. In spite of the difference in their individual rewards, Jane feels that she and Wendy are being treated fairly by the company. Jane reasons that Wendy has more education, more experience with the company, and more responsibility—and, therefore, that Wendy deserves her proportionately greater reward in terms of salary and vacation. This difference is not only acceptable to Jane but even pleases her, because it presents a future to which Jane aspires. Wendy's status demonstrates to Jane that rewards increase as contributions increase. Put simply, Jane is motivated to perform by the system of justice that is in place in the company.

INSIGHT 77	To estimate fairness, we make comparisons between our situation and that of others.

Your Turn	

Describe an individual or group with whom you make comparisons in the process of deciding the fairness with which you are treated in your school or work life. How did you select this person or group for comparison?

Because this system seems rational and motivating to us, we go to great lengths to keep it intact. If the system seems out of balance, we make adjustments to one or more of its components.

Adjusting our reward. If we feel that we are being treated unfairly in comparison to others, we might redefine our reward in some way to restore the balance. "Well, I don't get paid what I should," we might say, "but my boss is flexible when it comes to days when my child care falls through. I guess it all evens out." Here's another version of our attempt to redefine our reward: "I don't earn much as a tenured teacher, but my job is secure. By contrast, an administrator earns a bigger salary but can be fired at any time. It's a fair trade-off, I think."

INSIGHT 78	If we feel the fairness equation is out of balance, we might attempt to repair it by adjusting our estimate of our reward.

What is the downside of making a mental adjustment in our reward as a way of restoring the fairness equation? Draw from your personal experience if possible.

Adjusting our contribution. We also can attempt to balance the fairness equation by reconceptualizing (or reinventing) what we give to the company: "I don't like the fact that managers earn so much more than we supervisors do, but I guess it's fair in the long run because as a supervisor, I have an 8 to 5 union job. When the whistle blows, I go home. Managers aren't in the union, so they have to work as long as it takes, sometimes even weekends." Here's another version of adjusting the contribution portion of the equation: "I've only been with the company for a year. Even though I work as hard as the guy next to me, he has been here for 5 years. It's only fair that he gets more pay, considering what he has contributed over those years."

If the fairness equation seems unbalanced, we can attempt to alter our contribution.   **INSIGHT 79**

What is the downside of adjusting our estimate of our contribution as a way of restoring the balance of the fairness equation? Draw from your personal experience where possible.

Adjusting their reward. When we fail to restore justice (in our view) by altering our side of the equation, we can make changes in the other person's side of the formula: "They might seem like they're earning a lot more than I do, but their salary puts them in a higher tax bracket and they have to spend a lot on business suits. Their situation isn't as sweet as it seems." Another adjustment attempt: "My supervisor makes a lot more than I do and doesn't have to work as hard as I do. But I get the use of a company car for my sales calls. No one bothers me if I also use the car for a lot of personal travel, like everyone else in my group does. My supervisor doesn't get a company car. That's got to be at least a few thousand bucks out of his column and into mine."

| **INSIGHT 80** | If the fairness equation seems out of balance, we can attempt to adjust the reward of the comparison party. |

| **Your Turn** | |

What is the downside of adjusting the reward of the comparison party in our attempt to restore balance to the fairness equation? Draw on your personal experience where possible.

Adjusting their contribution. This change is perhaps the most familiar in reinterpreting equity in organizations: "My boss earns twice what I do, but look at her life! She's always stressed out by work and gets called at all hours of the night and on weekends for emergencies of one kind or another. Her job is no piece of cake!" Here's another version of the same kind of adjustment: "The men in my work group earn more than the women, but they are the ones who are usually asked to travel on weekends. When you figure it all out on an hourly basis, we're all compensated about the same."

The purpose of showing these mental games is to demonstrate how desperately we need and want to find fairness, by our definition, at the heart of our work arrangement with our employer. We do not want to feel that some workers are lucky and that we are not. We are motivated to give our best to our organizations when we believe that people are getting what they deserve.

| **INSIGHT 81** | If the fairness equation seems out of balance, we can attempt to repair it by adjusting the contributions of the comparison party. |

| **Your Turn** | |

What is the downside of attempting to adjust the contributions of the comparison party in our efforts to repair the balance of the fairness equation?

EXPERIENCING COGNITIVE DISSONANCE

So urgent is our general need to believe in fair rewards that we turn off our ability to see, hear, or think about information that contradicts our illusion of equity. When a direct short circuit occurs between what we believe to be true and what we observe to be true, "cognitive dissonance" occurs—much as harmonic dissonance results from two music pitches that clash when sounded together. We respond to this irritating mental noise by trying to quiet it, usually in one or more of the following ways.

Disbelief. When our sense of fairness is threatened, we can deny the threat entirely and make the cognitive dissonance go away: "I don't believe the top salespeople are earning more than the vice presidents in this company. That's just a myth to keep the sales-people working hard." Or: "That rumor about three people getting perfect scores on the final exam is untrue. I got a B and the instructor told me it was one of the better grades."

Selection. To make what we are hearing more palatable, we often take what we like and discard the rest: "Frank got the job instead of me because he's been here longer. That's the beginning and end of the story." Or: "Sally got a bigger bonus than the rest of us because the boss found out about her eldercare situation with her father. She needs the money more than we do."

Recasting. We also act to resolve cognitive dissonance by recasting or repositioning the entire message: "He was promoted to vice president, but it was one of those cases of being demoted by promotion. They had to find a polite way to get him out of our division before he did more damage, so they just promoted him." Or: "She has risen much too quickly in this company for someone with her limited skills. It's obvious she's sleeping with the boss."

Why go to the trouble of such mental gymnastics to preserve some sense of equity in our work relations? We do so because the alternative, we fear, is demotivating in the extreme: admitting that others have it better than we do through no merit of their own, but simply by luck. We feel foolish giving our best effort when that work doesn't result in some deserved reward in a larger system of equity. The idea that we, in our professional lives, are like leaves being blown about chaotically in a senseless maelstrom is abhorrent to us. Like Einstein, we deeply want to believe that "God does not play dice."

Cognitive dissonance prevents us from hearing information that contradicts our preferences or beliefs.	**INSIGHT 82**

Your Turn

Tell about a time when you received news you did not want to hear. Did you experience cognitive dissonance? How did you react?

FINDING MOTIVATION WHEN THE SCALES ARE TIPPED AGAINST US

To this point, we have seen that (a) we are motivated by the equity of the reward system in an organization; and (b) when such equity does not exist, we play elaborate mental games to pretend it does exist. If that discussion seems incomplete and unsatisfying to you, we agree.

Adults are entirely capable of recognizing the injustice of a reward system without allowing that recognition to rob them of motivation or send them into false and silly efforts to rewrite history. Here's how one employee faced up to a lack of equity in her work situation without caving in to despair or retreating to self-serving illusions.

Gwen had worked for 2 years in the training department of a large manufacturing company. When the company faced a shortfall in earnings per share for its stock, top management decided to boost apparent earnings by reducing the amount spent for salaries. The training department was hit especially hard. Gwen and five other trainers were given the option of quitting or working part time (20 hours) at a 50 percent reduction in pay. The jobs of three trainers who had worked with the company for less than a year were left untouched, as were the jobs of the four training supervisors and the training director. Gwen and her five coworkers received no explanation about why their positions were singled out for drastic cutbacks. As far as Gwen could discover, the company move had nothing to do with performance evaluations—hers were superior, and better in fact than the newer trainers whose jobs had not been cut. Over lunch, several of Gwen's coworkers expressed their theories of why some jobs had been cut and not others: "Those new trainers have been kissing up to the supervisors for months. Besides, the salaries of the new trainers are less than ours were, so they're cheaper to keep on. Management probably knew that the six of us would have to be promoted soon, because our performance evaluations have all been so good." Gwen listened to these "explanations" and others without saying much. When she went home, she had time to think about her own thoughts and feelings about the situation: "I don't think the cutbacks were fairly distributed. I don't think I am being treated fairly, considering what I have given to the company in relation to others. So, the bottom line is that life in this case isn't fair. The question is what to do about it. I can complain about the inequity to my manager, but he is not going to reverse his decision. I can sit around with my friends and make up fairy tales about why we got the short end of the stick, or I can keep unfairness from killing my motivation for a successful career in training."

To her credit, Gwen took that last alternative. Without hanging her head or resolving to get even, she agreed to work part time for the company so long as she was also free to work part time elsewhere. Within a few months, that additional part-time work for another company turned into a full-time job for a considerably larger salary than Gwen was earning in her previous full-time days with her original company. Gwen came out on top in this situation because she did not need to believe that the work world was fair in order to pursue her own interests in a motivated way.

"What kept me going," says Gwen, "was my inner confidence that I was a talented trainer and that companies needed that talent. I was motivated by the belief that I was good, not that companies were fair."

Wanting fairness and working for fairness should not make it impossible for us to seek our interests in environments where fairness is lacking.	**INSIGHT 83**

Your Turn
Describe how you dealt with a situation in which fairness could not be established or restored. What motivated you in this kind of environment?

MAKING THE BEST OF BROKEN SCALES

Certainly, it would be more pleasant if the reward systems of companies and other organizations kept us motivated by fair treatment. Without giving up our understandable need to find such treatment and our right to object when we don't receive it, we also have to prepare ourselves as survivors for a work world rife with inequities. If unfairness sends us running home like a kid whose ball has been stolen, we are giving up our power as individuals to those who foster such inequity. To defeat us professionally, these individuals simply have to create a climate of unfairness, knowing in advance that we wilt in such circumstances.

Or do we? Not if we have equipped ourselves with the many self-motivators described in these chapters. We move ahead in the work world, regretting the frequent inequity we find there and, when possible, attempting to rectify it. At no time do we allow workplace injustices to rob us of our motivation or direction. To do so would be unfair to ourselves.

Motivators based on fairness are only one in an array of many motivators available to each of us.	**INSIGHT 84**

Your Turn

Describe a situation when your primary motivator failed to sustain your effort and enthusiasm. Were you able to turn to a backup motivator? If so, what was it? If not, what backup motivator in hindsight could have served you well?

Summing Up

Fairness influences our willingness to pursue tasks and activities. That sense of fairness comes from our comparison of our contributions and rewards in relation to the contributions and rewards of others. When that comparison does not please us, we might make efforts (often wrongheaded) to adjust the comparison in our favor. Although we all seek fair environments in which to work and live, we must be prepared to pursue our interests in situations where fairness cannot be established or restored.

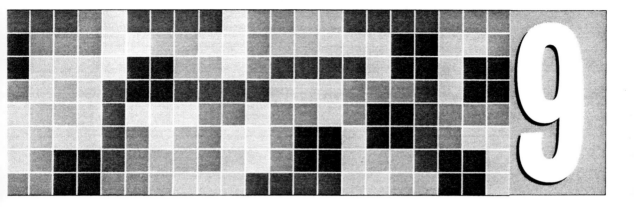

Overcoming Demotivators and Mapping Your Motivational Goals

GOALS

- Develop specific strategies for overcoming demotivators.

- Map out plans for using personal motivators to help you achieve your goals.

We began this book by describing 15 common demotivators—excuses, self-deceptions, and delaying tactics we all use from time to time to procrastinate. In this final chapter, we will look back to each of those demotivators from the perspective of what we have learned to this point. In each case, you will have "Your Turn" to write your own recipe for dealing with these derailing thoughts. Then you will help us write the conclusion to this book by supplying your ideas on how you can use the many self-motivators we have described.

LOOKING BACK AT DEMOTIVATORS WITH NEW EYES

No one can supply your personal way out of these demotivators except you. What we can do is raise a few questions you might want to consider before you write down in the "Your Turn" sections how you will handle these demotivators when they knock unexpectedly at your door.

1. "I just don't feel like it."
   - Are you in fact ill? If so, what should you do? If not, what should you do?
   - Tell in specific terms why you don't feel like it.
   - Describe what circumstances would motivate you to feel like it. Can you create those circumstances?

Your Turn

Write a short script (as if talking to yourself) in which you try to overcome this demotivator. In other words, what will you say to yourself when this demotivating thought gets in your way?

---

2. "I would if I could."
   - Is this a true statement? If not, who or what is causing you to prevaricate?
   - What prevents you? Be specific.

Your Turn

Write a short script (as if talking to yourself) in which you try to overcome this demotivator. In other words, what will you say to yourself when this demotivating thought gets in your way?

---

3. "It's no use."
   - Says who? Is this your firm opinion?
   - What could change the situation? Be specific.
   - Why does it seem so hopeless?

Write a short script (as if talking to yourself) in which you try to overcome this demotivator. In other words, what will you say to yourself when this demotivating thought gets in your way?

4. "It's so difficult!"
   ■ Are all parts of the task equally difficult? Can you begin with an easier part?
   ■ Are you capable of meeting this challenge?
   ■ What resources can you draw upon in reducing the difficulty of the task?

Write a short script (as if talking to yourself) in which you try to overcome this demotivator. In other words, what will you say to yourself when this demotivating thought gets in your way?

5. "I'm too busy."
   ■ Tell exactly what you are too busy to do.
   ■ What other activities keep you from taking on this task? Can you rearrange your schedule somewhat?
   ■ Would others believe that you are too busy if they knew specifically how you spend your time?

Write a short script (as if talking to yourself) in which you try to overcome this demotivator. In other words, what will you say to yourself when this demotivating thought gets in your way?

6. "I've done that before."
   ■ Are some aspects of this task new?
   ■ Can you use past experience to perform this task?
   ■ Do you feel you are stagnating or moving backward by doing this task? Is that in fact the case?

Your Turn

Write a short script (as if talking to yourself) in which you try to overcome this demotivator. In other words, what will you say to yourself when this demotivating thought gets in your way?

7. "Let someone else do it this time."
   - Are you annoyed at being asked to do this task? At whom are you irritated and why?
   - If that annoyance were not present, how would you feel about doing this task?
   - Did you do the task well the last time?

Your Turn

Write a short script (as if talking to yourself) in which you try to overcome this demotivator. In other words, what will you say to yourself when this demotivating thought gets in your way?

8. "What would they say?"
   - Tell exactly who "they" are.
   - Why do you care so much about their opinions and feelings?
   - How do you feel apart from the feelings of others?

Your Turn

Write a short script (as if talking to yourself) in which you try to overcome this demotivator. In other words, what will you say to yourself when this demotivating thought gets in your way?

9. "I'll do it later."
   - Is this a true statement or a delaying tactic?
   - If the statement is true, when will you do it?
   - Tell what advantage you gain in doing the job later rather than now.

Your Turn

Write a short script (as if talking to yourself) in which you try to overcome this demotivator. In other words, what will you say to yourself when this demotivating thought gets in your way?

10. "It's not worth it."
   - What is it worth to others? Be specific.
   - Does their perspective on the task influence your attitude?
   - In your mind, what would create worth for this task or activity?

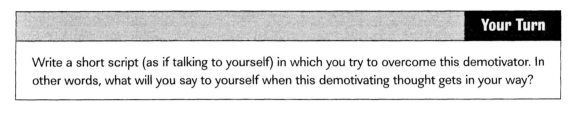

Your Turn

Write a short script (as if talking to yourself) in which you try to overcome this demotivator. In other words, what will you say to yourself when this demotivating thought gets in your way?

11. "It's not fair."
   - Explain what you mean by the term *fair*.
   - Is there any way you can increase the fairness you feel is lacking?
   - Does the lack of fairness prevent you from doing what you want?

Your Turn

Write a short script (as if talking to yourself) in which you try to overcome this demotivator. In other words, what will you say to yourself when this demotivating thought gets in your way?

12. "It's not my job."
   - Describe your job.
   - Who or what binds you to that job description?
   - Could you do this task or activity if you wanted to?

Your Turn

Write a short script (as if talking to yourself) in which you try to overcome this demotivator. In other words, what will you say to yourself when this demotivating thought gets in your way?

13. "I wouldn't lift a finger for him!"
   - Explain your angry feelings.
   - If those feelings did not exist, how would you feel about doing this task or activity?
   - What could you gain by doing this activity? Who will suffer if you do not do this activity?

Your Turn

Write a short script (as if talking to yourself) in which you try to overcome this demotivator. In other words, what will you say to yourself when this demotivating thought gets in your way?

14. "If I do this, they will expect more."
    - Who are "they"? Be specific.
    - Explain how you know they will expect more.
    - What would assure you that they will not expect more?

Your Turn

Write a short script (as if talking to yourself) in which you try to overcome this demotivator. In other words, what will you say to yourself when this demotivating thought gets in your way?

15. "I don't like working with them."
    - Identify "them."
    - Why do you dislike working with them?
    - Do you want these feelings to keep you from doing this task or activity?

Your Turn

Write a short script (as if talking to yourself) in which you try to overcome this demotivator. In other words, what will you say to yourself when this demotivating thought gets in your way?

MAPPING YOUR PERSONAL MOTIVATORS

A map shows locations and how to get there. Your map of personal motivators will specify "locations"—that is, metaphorical places you would like to be in your personal or professional life—and how to get there—that is, motivators that you believe will work for you. In each case, you are asked to supply a back-up motivator in case your first choice misfires or fails to sustain you all the way to your goal. To choose motivators, feel free to glance back through the pages of this book. An example is provided to make clear how to map your motivators.

Location 1: Where I want to be [in a leadership role in an organization at school or work]

What will motivate me to get there? Motivator 1: [Expectation—I really believe this experience will be good for me and my career path.]

Motivator 2: [Outside feelings of my parents and teachers—it will bring me pleasure to tell them about my position of responsibility.]

Location 2: Where I want to be
Motivator 1:
Motivator 2:

Location 3: Where I want to be
Motivator 1:
Motivator 2:

Location 4: Where I want to be
Motivator 1:
Motivator 2:

Location 5: Where I want to be
Motivator 1:
Motivator 2:

Location 6: Where I want to be
Motivator 1:
Motivator 2:

Location 7: Where I want to be
Motivator 1:
Motivator 2:

Location 8: Where I want to be
Motivator 1:
Motivator 2:

Location 9: Where I want to be
Motivator 1:
Motivator 2:

Location 10: Where I want to be
Motivator 1:
Motivator 2:

Summing Up

We can overcome the influence of demotivators by learning to "talk back" to them when they crop up to interfere with our goals and best interests. By naming our specific goals (or "locations where we would like to be") and planning appropriate motivators to help us reach those goals, we equip ourselves with the tools to meet challenges and achieve our dreams.

Recommended Reading

Blanchard, K. H. et al. *Gung Ho! Turn On the People in Any Organization*. New York: William Morrow, 1997

Blanchard, K. H. *The Little Book of Coaching: Motivating People to Be Winners*. New York: Harperbusiness, 2001.

Buckingham, M. et al. *Now, Discover Your Strengths*. New York: Free Press, 2001

Durand, David. *Perpetual Motivation*. New York: ProBalance, 2000.

Keller, Jeff. *Attitude Is Everything*. New York: Attitude Is Everything, Inc., 1999.

Maslow, A. H. et al. *Motivation and Personality*. Reading, MA: Addison-Wesley, 1987.

McCoy, Thomas. *Compensation and Motivation*. New York: AMACOM, 1992.

Mink, Oscar et al. *Developing High Performance People*. New York: Perseus Press, 1993

Nohria, Nitin. *Driven: The Four Key Drives to Understanding Why We Choose to Do What We Do*. San Francisco: Jossey-Bass, 2001.

Thomas, K. W. *Intrinsic Motivation at Work*. New York: Berrett-Koehler Publishers, 2000.

Whitmore, John. *Coaching for Performance*. New York: Nicholas Brealey, 1996.

Worman, David. *Motivating Without Money*. New York: Business by Phone, 1999.

Index

In this index, page numbers in *italics* designate illustrations. *See also* cross-references designate related topics or more detailed subentries.